SACRED
COMMERCE

SACRED COMMERCE

A BLUEPRINT FOR A NEW HUMANITY

2ND EDITION

AYMAN SAWAF &
ROWAN GABRIELLE

———————————— THE SACRED COMMERCE SERIES ————————————

© 2014 by Ayman Sawaf and Rowan Gabrielle

SacredCommerce.com

Published by EQ Enterprises
PO Box 719, Ojai, CA 93024
EQEnterprises.com

Managing Publisher: Immanuel Otto
Editor: Zelly Restorick
Cover Artist: © Duncan Walker (iStockPhoto.com)
Cover and Layout Designer: Bill Morosi
Copy Editor: Gary Sunshine

Up to 70% of this book was previously published in prior edition:
Sacred Commerce: The Rise of the Global Citizen (2007)

Library of Congress Cataloging-in-Publication Data
Sawaf, Ayman.
Sacred commerce : a blueprint for a new humanity / by
Ayman Sawaf and Rowan Gabrielle. -- 2nd edition.
pages cm
LCCN 2014950270
ISBN 978-0-9906987-0-8
1. Commerce. 2. Globalization. 3. Social evolution.
I. Gabrielle, Rowan. II. Title.

HF1008.S29 2014   382
QBI14-600156

DEDICATION

We dedicate this book to two very important people in our lives.

Nick Hart-Williams, Rowan's father, who showed Rowan that commerce could be different and encouraged her to be comfortable within the world of business from an early age.

We also dedicate this book to our middle son, Aziz Sawaf, for the Beauty, Goodness, and Truth he exudes and in recognition of his exceptional self-determination.

ACKNOWLEDGMENTS

We would like to thank our dear friend Kevin Ryerson for taking us to Egypt and introducing us to the ancient lineage of the Merchant Priesthood and the stories of their influence over Commerce throughout history. Without these stories and his "Drop of Joy" technique, this book would not exist.

Our deepest gratitude to our collaborators, Roger Housden, Geralyn Gendreau, and Zelly Restorick, all exceptional authors in their own right. We appreciate their eloquence, skills, and everything they have added to this project.

Lots of love to Immanuel Otto for catching the wave of Sacred Commerce and for grabbing hold of the baton with dedication and leadership. He has been pivotal in the production of the new edition of this book — and the accompanying training program and social network. We thank him for his belief in us and for his focus and excellent work.

We also thank our family and friends, who have helped and inspired us along the way — with special thanks to Christopher Hills, Jach Pursel, Hellmut Wolf, and our son, Azlan, who reminded us of the ways of the Magical Child.

Ayman and Rowan

TABLE OF CONTENTS

FOREWORD

"Yesterday I was clever. I wanted to change the world.
Today I am wise. I am changing myself."

— RUMI

Jean Erdman, wife of mythologist Joseph Campbell — who is known by most for coining the term "Hero's Journey" and for advising his students to "follow your bliss" — once said: "The way of the mystic and the way of the artist are related, except that the mystic doesn't have a craft."

This statement has remained with me since I first read it in the early nineties, motivating and underscoring every personal and professional choice along the way. I did not choose the path of an artist, per se, but of publishing for the artist in each of us — the one who is ultimately crafting the masterpiece of a life well lived. I used to wonder at this seeming dichotomy — being so interested in the arts, yet being pulled more in the direction of business. That was until I discovered *Sacred Commerce*.

When I read the first edition of this book, I immediately recognized that Rowan and Ayman were advocating for a similarly inspired approach — enlightening business leaders by helping them embody the spirit of being a *mystic with a craft* in the realm of commerce.

And enlighten we must! Inspired and creative contributions from the arena of commerce are needed more than ever. If we are to survive and thrive through the monumental cultural and environmental transition in which our planet is currently engaged, humanity must become aware of and act out of the deeper dimensions of interconnectedness that fuel and drive our greatest potentials — our inherent spiritual nature. The approach advocated for in these pages can activate this in our species en masse.

How does this "Sacred Commerce" thing change the world, though? And does it actually make it better?

What you'll come to learn from this approach is that we're not trying to improve on the old world. We're rebooting it with an entirely new operating system! We are co-creating a new world from the level of the quantum field on up.

In this revised and expanded edition, you'll discover a practical and easy-to-use template for *personal transformation* that is simultaneously specific and open source. Any individual, teacher, or organization can pick it up and modify it according to their own culture and spiritual inclinations.

In addition to unique and significant contributions to the exploration of Emotional Intelligence, one of the threads that make this book a classic is the insightful telling of the poetic and mystical tale of the Merchant Priesthood of ancient Egypt. The narrative both preserves and perpetuates wise jewels of antiquity by establishing an anchor to our world cultural heritage and mythical past that nurtures a *miracle-minded* space in us where the practical skills we need to develop as an *emotionally intelligent* global community can find relevance and purpose.

Inventor and futurist Buckminster Fuller endeavored to determine and document what one individual alone could achieve toward societal and planetary change. He used a simple metaphor to inspire and motivate himself and others:

"Something hit me very hard once, thinking about what one little man could do. Think of the *Queen Mary* — the whole ship goes by and then comes the rudder. And there's a tiny thing at the edge of the rudder called a trim tab. It's a miniature rudder. Just moving the little trim tab builds a low pressure that pulls the rudder around. Takes almost no effort at all. So I said that the little individual can be a trim tab. Society thinks it's going right by you, that it's left you altogether. But if you're doing dynamic things mentally, the fact is that you can just put your foot out like that and the whole big ship of state is going to turn. So I said, call me 'Trim Tab.'"

It is my sincerest hope that this book authentically connects you with the information, experience, and techniques necessary to evoke your own Trim Tab nature, so that you may purposefully move into your position as a primary healing force on this planet.

Thank you,

Immanuel Otto, M.A., K.T.S.
Managing Director, SacredCommerce.com

INTRODUCTION

"There is an almost sensual longing for communion
with others who have a large vision. The immense
fulfillment of the friendships between those engaged
in furthering the evolution of consciousness has
a quality almost impossible to describe."
— Pierre Teilhard de Chardin

Much of what constitutes successful and happy relationships, more than the influence of race, creed, or family, is a shared value system; a way of looking at the world almost as if you are looking through the eyes of the same soul. For us, it was a mutual love of business and spirituality that initially drew us to each other. Although we first met as competitors in the field of super foods, we soon joined forces in a collaboration that has subsequently grown to encompass everything we do.

This is our story, the evolving blueprint of how we want to live, love, and do business, which we share with you along with the hope that you will find within it your story. The storytellers in us encourage you to approach this book as you might a romantic novel, where fact and fantasy are seamlessly interwoven, allowing the concepts and images to nurture and inspire you. This is not designed to be a factual account of history or science, although the stories contained herein may give you new insight into humanity's past and inspire you to *"party-cipate,"* as we like to say, in the co-creation of a brilliant future.

In this book, we have expanded and built upon the Four Cornerstone Model, defined in the international best seller, *Executive EQ: Emotional Intelligence in Leadership and Organizations,* which Ayman co-authored with Dr. Robert Cooper. This was a lengthy text, full of studies, statistics, and exercises. With *Sacred Commerce,* however, we wanted to create a short and magical read, sharing with you beautiful and enchanting stories, which we envision will change how we all do business and live our lives.

This lyrical look at the evolution of commerce began as a collaboration with our dear friend Kevin Ryerson, who not only united us in an ancient Celtic ceremony inside Stonehenge, but just a few months later guided us through Egypt for our honeymoon, exploring the sacred sites and eventually leading us to a discovery that would change the course of our lives.

It was on this tour that we were first introduced to the Merchant Priesthood of old Egypt. An expert in mythology and history, Kevin has a specific interest in Egyptian myths and mysticism, which he generously shared with us, lighting a flame that continues to burn to this day.

While in the Temple of Isis in Philae, the area known as "the Jewel of the Nile," we briefly separated from the group. Out of nowhere, two Egyptian men walked up to us and, in broken English, asked if we wanted to have our picture taken next to a nearby square stone, upon which a figure was carved. Thinking they were after a tip, Ayman, a native speaker of Arabic, firmly replied, "Laa shukran." However, the two men persisted, refusing to take "no" for an answer. "We don't want your money," one of the men said indignantly. "We just want to take your picture," said the other. "Here, please, stand here," he added, pointing again to the square stone. Finally, in an effort to just get rid of them, we agreed and stood beside the stone to have our photo taken. The men then handed the camera back to us and disappeared.

On the way out, we told Kevin about this odd interaction involving the two men and showed him the stone where we had posed for the picture. Knowing we were both entrepreneurs, a big smile spread across his face. "That's not just any stone," he said, "look again. Do you know who that is?" We spoke together, saying, "No." "This is the Egyptian god, Bes, the god of commerce," explained Kevin. "He is the god who oversaw the Merchant Priesthood." We both smiled and looked at each other, filled with curiosity and wonder.

Merchant Priesthood? Neither of us had ever heard of a Merchant Priest. We'd known that there were Temple Priests, Healing Priests, and Celebration Priests, but Merchant Priests? Over time, Kevin shared many stories with us about the Merchant Priesthood and we, in turn, did a good bit of research into the subject, gathering anecdotal evidence from a variety of sources. We will review these stories in more detail in Part Two.

What fascinated us from the start was the idea that commerce could be a vehicle to raise consciousness, as well as a spiritual path towards self-realization. Could commerce — that intrinsic and basic function of exchanging information, goods, and services — actually lift a culture to a level of sacredness that might otherwise not be attained, as well as put those who practice it on an accelerated growth trajectory? This idea made perfect sense to us and rang through our minds like a clarifying bell whose echoes are as bright and clear today as when we first heard it sing.

Over the years the concept of Sacred Commerce has gone through many levels of refinement, integrating the input of many wise friends, colleagues, and readers of the previous edition. We invite you to add your voice by visiting the network — *SacredCommerce.com* — with the aim of developing and growing this meme together. There are many other reasons to visit the Sacred Commerce network, including trainings, articles, interactive blogs and vlogs, discussion groups, global meditations, and the connection with like-minded people.

We will continue to publish updated and enhanced editions, including the most relevant and exciting additions that *you* contribute. This will allow the book to remain fresh and relevant throughout our quickly changing times. The concept and practice of Sacred Commerce will be given life and breath by you, allowing it to grow faster than if we tried to "own" or "lead" it ourselves.

That said, we take deeply to heart our roles as germinal and fully invested stewards of this movement. In that spirit, we'd like to shed some light on common themes we encounter when people open this book with preconceived ideas inspired by simply reading the words "sacred commerce." The most common are based in an expectation that *Sacred Commerce* be a critique of sorts, a social commentary on the current systems of commerce — many of which are widely declared among enlightened/progressive circles to be outdated, broken, corrupt, and worse. While we clearly acknowledge the many problems looming worldwide, our particular inspiration is grounded in a commitment to inner growth and spirituality. It is a call to acknowledge that the entirety of the agreements and systems we've created externally — including corrupt financial systems and power hierarchies — is a hyper-correlative mirror of our individual and collective inner lives and values.

A key realization in our process is that the central principle and "engine" of culture is no longer religion or politics, as has been the case in the past. Like it or not, commerce has become the primary force propelling our species and human society forward. We are currently witnessing a commerce-centric (r)evolution, a whole new form of "conscious capitalism," whereby business transactions the world over are becoming the main conduit of social and cultural evolution.

In recent years, many new business concepts have been suggested and developed, such as sustainable business, conscious commerce, the gift economy, alternative currency (like Bitcoin), crowd-funding, and maybe soon, as advocated by Dr. Muhammad Yunis, a stock market for social entrepreneurs. People often ask us which one we support and our answer is that they are all systems or tools and, as such, are open to abuse. It is the way we, as individuals, use them that makes them constructive or destructive. Emotional Intelligence is key to the new business paradigm, whatever the system, which is why we consider it foundational to Sacred Commerce. Consequently, we feel most inclined to foster a conversation around refining the tool makers' spirits and values and allowing the various tools we will need to emerge naturally out of the rich soil of a truly enlightened global business culture.

Some readers may search through these pages for affirmation of the idea that we must band together and root out the governing elite and hold them accountable for what one of our more notable early reviewers of this edition referred to as: "the inherent 'legalized' corruption of our current money and banking system — i.e. taxation, fiat money, fractional reserve, central banking, debt-based economy, bailouts, subsidies, state protected monopolies on money and force, etc." We neither support this small majority or vilify them. We are not naive or blind to the fact that the abundance of this planet is not being equitably shared and that the institutional violence of our current system has caused unthinkable suffering throughout the world. However, our focus is to suggest that when these leaders are truly no longer needed, they'll be gone not long after the advent of a mass scale awakening of *individuals* worldwide taking more responsibility upon themselves to create and adhere to new agreements for coexisting on this planet.

Ultimately, we welcome many expressions of this conversation… *and* will always seek to ground the many different and complementary streams in the insight that nothing outside of us will change until we change from within first. And, of course, inspired and meaningful action will follow. As the old Zen saying goes: "After enlightenment, chop wood, carry water."

Returning to the subject of Emotional Intelligence, as part of Ayman's personal healing journey years ago, he discovered that his lack of understanding about his feelings and emotions was the source of his bad health, depression, and lack of joy and happiness in his life.

Ayman also became very aware that Emotional Intelligence had played no part in his education and quickly came to the realization that our school system was dysfunctional and needed to change.

Researching different educational paradigms, Ayman became very excited to learn about Steiner, Montessori, and alternative charter schools. Along with other inspired teachers and scientists, he began developing and investing in a new school system he believed would solve the problem. Sharing this with one of his closest friends, he was shocked and hurt when the friend suggested that his idea — although well intentioned — was a bit arrogant and that he was still seeing life through the chauvinistic lens of competition: simply trying to create a new system that would compete with other systems. Acknowledging that his idea was worthwhile and of value, the friend suggested the alternative of infusing the existing systems with innovative learning tools and programs about emotions, thereby changing the system from within.

Soon after this, Ayman coined the term "Emotional Literacy" and through his company, *Enchanté Entertainment* — now called *Kids EQ* — he created the first curriculum to teach this subject both at home and in schools. His other approach would surely have failed, whereas now, Emotional Literacy has entered mainstream education systems worldwide — private, public, charter, military, and religious — and will very soon be taught in equal partnership with intellectual literacy. In the home, parents are also learning the principles of Emotional Literacy alongside their children, as a cornerstone of the new conscious parenting paradigm. In this way, a whole new generation of young adults is emerging, who are more balanced, healthier, more success-ful, and more at peace with themselves and the world.

Just as Ayman discovered that the missing link in our edu-cation system was Emotional Literacy, we discovered that in the world of business, Emotional Intelligence — one of the keys to spirituality and an expression of the feminine — is similarly missing. Chauvinism has stripped the sacred and the feminine from nearly all aspects of our lives where they are most needed, making the loss of them unsustainably painful.

The Merchant Priest/Priestess is reawakening in all of us. The wisdom of Sacred Commerce is being passed to renaissance men and women all over the world, in every culture and religion. Our dream is that the concept will become a lifestyle, not just a business activity — and that the growing self-identified constituency of the emergent Global Citizen movement will grab hold of this baton as one of its core organizing principles.

Sacred Commerce is all about *you* changing *you*; evolv-ing the business world one person at a time. Using a system guided by spirituality — with the pursuit of Beauty, Goodness, and Truth at the core of all business endeavors and activities — is truly the key to unlocking the Sacred in Commerce.

In joy,
Ayman and Rowan

(Editor's Note: As you read on, please note that when the text switches to the first person, it is Ayman — when "we" is used, it is Ayman and Rowan.)

PART ONE

SACRED COMMERCE

THE GIFT

REVERED AS A SPIRITUAL PATH, COMMERCE EMERGED LONG ago as a tool to advance mankind. Among the Merchant Priesthood of old Egypt, it was viewed as a Gift from the Goddess, sacred and balanced by its very nature. It was seen as a solution or a map to deal with the issues of survival, security, and community, the first three human needs per Maslow's Hierarchy of Needs (more on that later).

First and foremost, one of the greatest known benefits of Commerce is the ability to create **Abundance,** lifting people out of poverty and the needs of survival and security. This is evident in our society and history; there is little need for detailed explanation. By reducing the pain and suffering of the constant struggle just to survive, Abundance opens the door to other avenues of expression, such as relationships, creativity, and the pursuit of happiness and spirituality. Abundance is defined as "having access to the resources you need at the time you need them." It has nothing to do with stockpiling money or assets. In the context of Sacred Commerce, the emphasis of this Gift turns to the enjoyment and sharing of that Abundance, called **Prosperity**.

Every year, the leaders of the wealthiest nations in the world meet for an economic summit. During one such "G8" conference, considerable pressure was brought to bear on them to "forgive" poorer nations their debts. Moved to speak from a different perspective, Nelson Mandela addressed the issue at the G7 in 2005, essentially declining aid in favor of trade. "We need trade justice: no more subsidies and tariffs from the West that harm the exports and the people of Africa and the developing world." He went on to say, "We need help to build infrastructure so that Africa can take advantage of trading opportunities and be given a fair chance to compete in the world economy." Sourced via *The Guardian*.

Mandela's words point out the difference between sympathy and empathy — between *feeling sorry for someone* and *feeling their pain or struggle*. The former gives rise to pity, which is the word used to define sympathy in the dictionary. A sympathizer risks getting sucked into another's suffering, because pity is an emotion that works like an anesthetic, numbing us to the reality at hand and robbing us of the ability to change anything. Whereas, with empathy, we can feel someone's sorrow instead of feeling sorry for him or her, allowing us to raise the bar to compassion, evoking a very different response. Compassion's call to action is more likely to be one of caring or "tough love" that generates Right Action and a proactive intervention to lift another out of despair and defeat. The empathic response holds a higher Resonance, as it meets the person where he or she is, whereas sympathy can reinforce the stance of both the "victim" and the "martyr," with one person standing outside and above another and showering guilt, pity, and condolences over the other's distress.

From Mandela's perspective, trade is one of the remedies that can resolve the issue of poverty, rather than simply putting a Band-Aid over the problem. His call to action is one of proactive compassion rather than passive pity. Trade is an intervention that addresses the problem and provides a practical solution. Aid, on the other hand, although offered with beautiful intention, reinforces the problem by keeping impoverished people dependent, not unlike handing a starving person a trout, but withholding the secret of how to bait a hook. Trade, in Africa's case, is one of the needed "solution sets" that addresses both poverty and, simultaneously, violence.

Commerce has also been one of the most significant deterrents to war. Historically, the primary means by which both people and nations solved problems of limited resources was through taking what they needed — often by force. Neighbor attacked neighbor, tribe attacked tribe, and country attacked country. Men stole each other's resources and assets and enslaved each other's women and children, all in the interest of expansion, wealth acquisition, and a conqueror's glory.

When we look at evolution as progressive stages that build on the strengths and resolve the shortcomings of what came before, we can understand the importance of this "warrior" stage. Cultural evolution reveals warrior consciousness as necessary, in order for small bands and tribes to grow and develop into agrarian kingdoms. It was not until a certain level of emotional maturity had started to percolate in people's minds and hearts that the concept of peace through negotiation and compromise became available to humanity. Until then, Commerce provided one of the only real antidotes to war, acting as a carrot leading to **peace**.

The European Union (EU) is an inspiring example of how Commerce can lead to — or is an agent of — Peace. Once bitter enemies who fought some of the bloodiest wars on any soil, European nations have united under a common market, currency, and trans-national vision. What started as a common market among six countries has given birth to the euro and the EU, an alliance of nearly thirty nations with more waiting to join.

Today, with a population twice as large as the US and on a similar landmass, the EU boasts the world's largest economy. The French still love to tease the English, of course, and the English are as wry as ever when it comes to lambasting the French — and yet, when the time comes, they get down to business, because business is the common thread that makes the European Union strong and affords them an enviable quality of life. With longer than average life spans, lower crime rates, far fewer prisons, less violence in society, and a clear movement away from religion toward spirituality, many Europeans are already enjoying the benefits of this emerging Global Citizenship.

That Commerce can bring former enemies together has also been demonstrated in American relations with China. When Richard Nixon went to China, ostensibly to watch the table tennis teams compete, he managed to also strike a number of business deals. At that time in history, the polarization between communism and democracy had wedged an ideological gap between the US and China that was far more difficult to cross than the Pacific Ocean separating the two countries. The "Ping-Pong strategy" opened the door for these archenemies to become instead co-conspirators in the name of Commerce. Trade agreements between the two countries in turn stimulated the exchange of culture. Today, we have a window into China that was not possible when the Great Wall was as blinding a barrier as the Iron

Curtain. Commerce was the initial bridge or stepping-stone and, although China may never embrace democracy as we do, more and more people are being lifted out of poverty and China has seen greater peace than ever before in its recent history.

Considering the power of Commerce as a deterrent against war and conflict, and having been born in the Middle East, I have always dreamed of peace in this region. As a solution to solving this problem, war has failed over and over again and has been the source of immense pain and suffering to millions of people — of all races, ages, and gender. I believe that if Israel and the Arab countries chose instead to engage in Commerce together, as has happened in other parts of the world, it would be entirely possible for peace to flourish. I feel deeply that the people do not know one another and many individuals and groups seem to concentrate only on what separates them from each other, as opposed to what unites them. Commerce is a tool — a Gift — that allows people to get to know one another.

Interestingly, the work of Dr. Muhammad Yunus, one of the first economists to sit in the company of Nelson Mandela, the Dalai Lama, Desmond Tutu, Mother Teresa, and others, has advanced the cause of peace worldwide. Interestingly, Dr. Yunus was not awarded an *economic* prize in 2006 for his work in microlending — which lifted millions of families from poverty to the middle class in his home country of Bangladesh and also around the world: he was awarded the world's most prestigious prize — the Nobel *Peace* Prize!

We've shown how Commerce can lead both the individual and society to Prosperity and Peace. What is not normally acknowledged or explored is how Commerce can be seen as an ally on our personal journey toward self-realization and conscious evolution.

As part of my own healing journey and a desire to express more of myself, I began composing and playing music. My fourth album had just been released, when a friend came to me saying that an associate of his had heard it and wanted to meet me. His name was Dr. Christopher Hills. When I looked at this striking man for the first time, I remember thinking he was some kind of Merlin-figure or wizard. I could see a great inner light beaming through his eyes. Later, I discovered he had written twenty-two books on spiritual philosophy and the science of consciousness and was a highly skilled and visionary entrepreneur. This meeting heralded a significant turning point in my life.

Let's look at Dr. Christopher Hills' experience as an example of this shift toward connecting Commerce with self-realization and conscious evolution. Hills traveled to India in the early 1960s to pursue enlightenment. As part of his initiation, he went walking from village to village with a begging bowl. He would often be surrounded by hundreds of starving children, pressing their own begging bowls toward his dirty robes. As he entered one particular village, he was literally swarmed by close to a hundred children. In that moment, he looked up to God and promised to find a solution to famine.

Over the years, he had occasion to meet many political and spiritual leaders in India. In an effort to take the science of yoga to the West, he initiated the first world yoga conference, inviting the most prominent yogis in India to attend. However, a power struggle ensued, as the various gurus battled over who would get the most time in the spotlight at the conference. Appalled by this behavior, Hills began to notice an alarming paradox. According to custom and the culture in India, a guru's followers were encouraged to donate to their spiritual teacher and guide. Many of these gurus had millions of followers. Starving, bedraggled devotees — whose bone-thin children had to beg in the streets and often died of malnutrition before reaching adulthood — would hand their meager income over to their guru, in the hope of being reborn to a more gracious life amongst an upper caste. It sadly reminded him of how many churches and organized religions in the West encourage or require their members to contribute a portion of their livelihood, in the hope of salvation, forgiveness, or access to God. A form of spiritual taxation. The behavior of the gurus not only angered Hills, it fired his passion to take action; he canceled the conference and flew home to California.

Once settled in the States, Hills started the University of the Trees, guiding his students spiritually and simultaneously helping them to create Abundance and Prosperity by developing a multitude of green and holistic businesses. This included the marketing of a newly discovered food supply called *Spirulina* (a super-food from the algae family), developed with the intention of addressing world famine. Hills founded the *Light Force Company,* as a vehicle designed to bring *Spirulina* to the world.

Multi-level marketing was a little-known business model at the time, outside of *Amway* and a few others, but Hills saw this model as a way to bring prosperity and higher consciousness to his students — and he succeeded. Although unfortunately over time, the concept of the multi-level business was corrupted and abused by those with greedy intentions, with many people being hurt and alienated, this well-intentioned idea is still used by many around the world in an honorable way.

By cultivating a nutrient-dense food source, Hills found a way to fulfill his sacred promise to address the issue of famine. Even the poorest countries could learn to grow *Spirulina* in ponds and have access to nutrition of the highest quality. Hills envisioned entire populations being lifted out of disease and famine with this type of support for their immune systems, along with a multitude of other benefits. From a joint business and spiritual perspective, by providing people with high-quality *Spirulina,* Hills and the *Light Force Company* gave people the chance to be self-employed and the opportunity for Right Livelihood. Many found independence that afforded them the freedom and extra time to explore their higher needs for creative expression and spiritual practice. Distributors began to enjoy an intangible and yet prized bonus, as the spiritual dimension of their lives began to grow and flourish. Hill's way of doing business planted a seed that has since bloomed into the practice we now call Sacred Commerce.

I recognized Hills' genius. What he had set out to do made perfect sense. When I saw the potential to make a lot of money, selling a product that solved a major human dilemma, while simultaneously supporting thousands in doing the same, the sense of disquiet, which had often accompanied my self-sense as a businessman, was soothed. Here was a better way. Engaging in Commerce need no longer be a dehumanizing activity. Hills had developed a potentially brilliant solution. I aligned fully with Hills' vision and we became business partners. What Christopher confirmed through his actions was that business could be used as a spiritual path — and as a way to raise the consciousness of the people practicing it, putting them on the trajectory of conscious evolution. The Merchant Priests of old Egypt had a deep understanding of this — and it is why they saw Commerce as a sacred practice. It offers us a spiritual path for when we are ready to undertake that ultimate spiritual adventure: *Coming home.*

All cultures have this leaving and returning home as one of the central themes in their mythologies. We leave Paradise and our sense of oneness with God and get lost in a wilderness, separated, apart, and alone. However, we are always given a map and the free will to return. Joseph Campbell named this essential archetypal pattern "The Hero's Journey." Whether we seek salvation, enlightenment, or the Promised Land, we are all involved in a similar process of returning home to the Divine.

The diagram below summarizes the many maps or psychological models of this Hero's Journey, using a rendition of Abraham Maslow's Hierarchy of Needs pyramid. Maslow's concept, simply put, is that human beings start by meeting their needs from the bottom up. As we meet our needs of survival, security, and belonging, a sense of happiness emerges that stretches us to pursue the higher needs of self-esteem, the expression of our creativity and productivity, knowing, and spirituality. It was Maslow's belief that we all have an integral, core desire to progress through this hierarchy and, although only a few people actually attain the goal of self-actualization, he felt the capability was within us all.

The Hierarchy of Needs

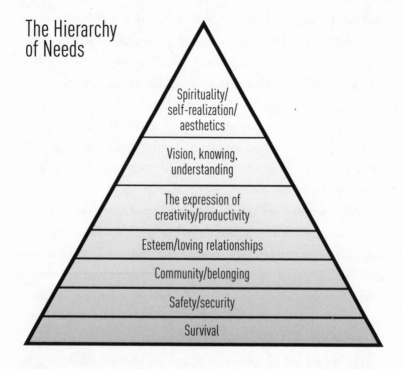

Spirituality/
self-realization/
aesthetics

Vision, knowing,
understanding

The expression of
creativity/productivity

Esteem/loving relationships

Community/belonging

Safety/security

Survival

Maslow's map is echoed by the Eastern concept of the seven Chakras, each representing different aspects of our physical, emotional, mental, and spiritual development. Another alternative map is offered later in this book, based on our own Hero's Journey and our exploration of the energy and information of emotions.

We've seen how Commerce provides a leg up by allowing us to rise above two of the most pressing human issues: poverty and war. We've climbed up from the base of the needs pyramid in Maslow's Hierarchy, where survival, safety, and community are our primary focus and concern, to the point where we are free to explore new horizons and look over the edge toward the future. While many mystics and individual seekers have experienced and met most of their human needs, now humanity as a whole is finally moving out of the sphere of primal needs into a global "Conscious Evolution." With a sufficient number of humans "coming of age" in terms of having completed the early stages of their personal development, the possibility of humanity evolving spiritually and consciously increases exponentially.

What do we mean by "Conscious Evolution"? To be "conscious" means to be "aware" and "evolution" is about becoming more of who we are. Conscious Evolution is therefore about being aware of who we are becoming and being able to direct that becoming more elegantly, in the pursuit of the highest need of spirituality.

"Biological Evolution" is an extremely long, slow process where progress is typically noted in terms of tens of thousands of years. It is a process that primarily uses a process of elimination and mutation to vault ahead and move beyond limitations and shortcomings. However, Conscious Evolution is unique, in that it puts the pioneer in full possession of his or her ability to act with awareness and intention to bring about desired changes and engineer forward movement, leading to the advancement of both our individual species and the biosphere as a whole.

Many problems and crises threaten our survival today — and it is the extent of the threat and the depth of the dysfunction that propels us to evolve as rapidly and comprehensively as possible. It was in the wake of the nuclear attacks on Nagasaki and Hiroshima that visionary author Barbara Marx Hubbard originally coined the term Conscious Evolution, recognizing that humans of our generation stand on a unique and precarious precipice.

According to scholar and philosopher Jean Houston PhD, this type of precipice is something of a cultural pressure cooker, often preceding sudden leaps ahead, as discussed at length in her book *Jump Time*. "Conscious Evolution is the evolution of evolution from unconscious to conscious. While consciousness has been evolving for billions of years, Conscious Evolution is new. It is part of the trajectory of human evolution, the canvas of choice before us now, as we recognize that we have come to possess powers that we used to attribute to the gods."

Although I'm still in the process of exploring the concept of Conscious Evolution, I believe there are some specific prerequisites needed to put us on this trajectory. One is consciously and elegantly using "Resonance causation" in our reality creation, where the future creates the present against the backdrop of the past. The other important key is evolving our relationship with the Divine from one of fear and love to one of Partnership and co-creation.

The old way of fixing and creating things through cause and effect is one form of causation, but it only partially explains how reality functions. The exceptions to the rule of cause and effect — and there are many — have normally been attributed to God, luck, magic, coincidence, or miracles. However, the latest advances in science and quantum physics are laying down the scientific foundation for the concept of Resonance causation, which has always been a part of our reality creation, albeit unconsciously.

Knowledge of this form of causation has resided in all great teachings both ancient and modern. Gandhi said: "You must be the change you want to see in the world." The Quran says: "Indeed, Allah will not change the condition of a people, until they change what is in themselves" (Quran 13:11). Socrates said: "Let him who would move the world, first move himself."

Science is now merely confirming what the ancients and the mystics have always known: our reality is subjective. We "create our reality" by causing it or by allowing it. Our *en*-vironment is only mirroring or reflecting our *in*-vironment; therefore, any change must start from within each one of us, as individuals. As we change our Resonance, so our reality changes, as it has no other option but to comply. (We will be exploring Resonance causation in much greater detail later in the book.)

Our current global problems are so vast, we simply cannot resolve them fast enough if we limit ourselves to the traditional concept of cause and effect. Many of our scientists and environmentalists already predict that there is not enough time remaining to ensure our survival and protect the planet from global disaster. Having bought into the cause and effect paradigm, hook, line, and sinker, we can see why they have reached this conclusion. In order to deal with the huge complexities of our current reality and to bring about a positive resolution, we urgently need the power-boost that comes with the shift from unconscious to Conscious Evolution.

So what happened to the Gift of Commerce? As we've said, up until the current era, evolution has marched human-ity along for the most part unaware and for the past two thousand years, this slow trudging forward has taken a dis-tinctly chauvinistic course. Scholar, writer, and social activist

Riane Eisler calls this the *androcentric paradigm*, a governance of social organization dominated by males or "the dominator model."

"Chauvinism" is defined as excessive or prejudiced loyalty to a particular gender, group, or cause. Although we have moved a long way from the extreme chauvinism of the recent past, it still permeates all of our senses and, if left unchecked, colors much of our lives.

With the rise of chauvinism, an authoritarian stance emerged that stripped humanity — and indeed, Commerce — of its sacred and feminine context, leading us to the unconscious exchange of goods and services that we experience today. What was once a sacred practice lost its soul and became brittle — with men becoming "busy-ness-men" and women turned into "sexy-taries."

Historically, the role of the Merchant Priest has been to work either overtly or behind the scenes, doing what they can to improve the human condition on its spiritual quest. This is their service to humanity. Their principal role and concern has always been to protect the divine Gift of Commerce, by creating and protecting an environment conducive to democratic principles and encouraging and maintaining the balance between the feminine and the masculine energies, thus enhancing the sacred in everything and keeping chauvinism at bay.

With its promise of equality and freedom, they knew that democracy was a prerequisite for the tools of Commerce — from the coin to the stock market — not something to be abused by one segment of society at the expense of another. The Gift of Commerce would rise when feminine and sacred values arose within a culture and then went underground, beneath the next wave of chauvinism. This is when some of the Merchant Priesthood, visionaries and renaissance men and women, formed secret societies to conceal their activities from the ruling class and avoid persecution. It should be noted here that these secret societies are not to be confused with the ones that are often blamed for the inequities in our current social agreements; and where overlap has occurred, it has often has been the case the society began with noble principles and participants, but were infiltrated and ultimately consumed by members with self-serving motivations based in greed for resources and power. That is why we now present Sacred Commerce as an "unsecret society" that can serve those of good conscience and faith in our species as we co-create our new world.

In order to maintain balance, both feminine and masculine principles need to be cherished and revered, not only within our society, but also within each of us as individuals. It is believed by some that the two hemispheres of the brain connect to the "sacred masculine" and the "sacred feminine" states of consciousness. Regardless of our gender, the right sphere represents the "feminine" and relates to the left-hand side of the body and the left hemisphere represents the "masculine," relating to the right-hand side of the body.

Throughout the history of old Egypt, it is possible to see the shifts between more feminine- and more masculine-influenced societies. When out of balance, the term "patriarchy" in this context is associated with war, invasion, aggression, control, dominance, authority, and force, whereas matriarchal systems are associated with times of peace, prosperity, and the intrinsic balance between the "masculine" and the "feminine" principles and the harmonious union between humanity, nature, and spirituality.

This pattern of shifting between patriarchal and matri-archal styles of social organization can be seen in many different cultures throughout our history. Currently, we live in a more patriarchal system of dominance and authority, conflict, disagreement, and power struggle. This affects every aspect of our lives, including our relationship with ourselves and the way we interrelate to each other, as individuals and groups. A sense of spiritual connection has been lost and it could be said that in terms of our communal Hero's Journey, we are in the wilderness.

Although the Gift of Commerce has been corrupted, it luckily has not been destroyed. It has created a positive impact on both the alleviation of poverty and the promo-tion of peace and, as the feminine and sacred values are reawakening and resurfacing within ourselves and our world, humanity is reaching a level of emotional maturity, whereby the Gift of Commerce will be able to deliver on its sacred promise as never before.

SACRED COMMERCE AND THE
____ FOURTH BOTTOM LINE ____

TRADE HAS EXISTED SINCE THE EARLY DAYS OF HUMAN HISTORY, but it was in ancient Egypt that it was first instituted as a sacred practice. Since then, it has reemerged in many forms, throughout every known civilization, bringing about the empowerment needed to evolve human societies.

Let us break down the term "Sacred Commerce" to clarify exactly what it means. "Sacred" is a Resonance or a synergy of many frequencies, especially those of Beauty, Enchantment, Love, and Mystery. (We will explore this in more detail later in the book.) "Commerce" means any exchange or transaction; it involves all of our day-to-day actions, not only those of a financial nature.

"Sacred Commerce" is the "*party-cipation*" of the community in the exchange of information, goods, and services that contributes to the revealing of the Divine (Beauty, Goodness, and Truth) in all — and where the bottom line is your spirituality.

There is a difference between spirituality and religion. Spirituality involves us in a unique and personal relationship with the Divine — or "All That Is" — whereas religion typically offers theology, dogma, and belief as the bridge between the individual and the Divine. The latter generally presupposes the individual's inability to commune directly with God or to merge with spiritual realities on your own. With spirituality, there are no prerequisites, no entry rules or regulations and no judges. It is, in truth, a part of your life, whether you are conscious of it or not. Spirituality — and for that matter, all world religions — view Beauty, Goodness, and Truth as being at the intrinsic core of all things, as well as being the light on our way back home. The ultimate goal is for these elevated spiritual states to become permanent traits; this is what is sometimes called "enlightenment."

Sacred Commerce lifts the concept of participation to its higher octave of *party-cipation.* This is a participation sourced in joy and celebration, with choice and responsibility at its core, versus a participation that is weighed down with duty and obligation, demands and expectations. It is a participation involving co-creation, where we share the success of that creation equally, yet take full responsibility for any shortcomings. After all, there is no one to blame.

Throughout our lives, we are constantly engaged in exchanges, communications, and interactions with other people in our sphere of influence. Psychiatrist Dr. Eric Berne, who, in the late 1950s, developed the concept of transactional analysis as a model for personal change and growth, called these exchanges "transactions."

The theory of transactional analysis also suggested that within each of us, there are different aspects of our psyche constantly engaging in internal dialogue, with or without our awareness — and that different parts of our multiple natures emerge, depending on the people we are with and the circumstances. We are therefore constantly communicating with others and ourselves throughout our lives, engaging in vast numbers of transactions.

Sacred Commerce was, of course, the domain of the Merchant Priest. Many people studied with the Merchant Priesthood purely to learn the skills of Emotional Intelligence or as they called it, "Inner Commerce." Inner Commerce is the Commerce between you and your unique personal Resonance and all its constituents, such as your emotions, your beliefs, thoughts, choices, and decisions. It is also the Commerce between you and all the different aspects of yourself, such as your inner child, your negative ego, your future Self, your Higher Self, and the Divine, as manifested in a myriad of ways, represented by everyone you meet and everything that crosses your path.

These students of the Merchant Priesthood returned home, infusing every aspect of their lives with this knowledge, creating loving and intimate relationships, prosperity, and a sense of community. Others, however, stayed in the Priesthood to further their studies, specializing in Emotional Alchemy, becoming the Merchant Priests.

Emotional Alchemy was a prerequisite for the Merchant Priests on their Hero's Journey, as well as in their practice of Sacred Commerce. It was necessary for them to understand and practice Inner Commerce, before they applied the principles outwardly in their service to humanity through business.

For a while now, in meditation at the end of every week, I have developed the practice of examining any transactions — or exchanges — that have triggered intense emotions within me. This involves a process of honest self-reflection and non-judgmental examination, looking at what needs processing and considering if any adjustments need to be made. Similarly, I explore my successes, congratulating myself and feeling grateful for the help I have received. This practice is equivalent to reviewing a weekly profit and loss (P&L) statement.

To my surprise, many years after my father died, my brother found an old journal from when our father was at Harvard Business School, detailing his own personal, emotional, and spiritual analysis of himself. On a regular basis, he would compile his Balance Sheet, detailing any areas for improvement and identifying and acknowledging his strengths and weaknesses. It was a record of his Assets and Liabilities. As with my own analysis, this wasn't a financial reckoning, rather an ongoing personal, emotional, and spiritual assessment.

Over the last twenty years, a business model has emerged which includes consciousness, awareness, and sustainability within Commerce, ending up with what is now known as "conscious commerce" or "sustainable business practice."

The old paradigm, whereby the bottom line, return on investment (ROI), simply meant how much cash flowed back into the hands of investors, has given way to the concept of the "Triple Bottom Line," a term coined by John Elkington in 1994 to describe the separate social, financial, and environmental bottom lines of companies.

The intention of the Triple Bottom Line of people, planet, and profit — also known as TBL, 3BL, and The Three Pillars — is to evolve the goal of sustainability and socially responsible business practices. In this model, the rate of return on investment is no longer measured only in cold, hard cash, but in more humane and balanced terms: return to the employees who help to create the profit, plus return to our planet and community in terms of sustainability and social responsibility. As of today, over 50% of the world's largest companies publish Triple Bottom Line reports. In these reports, the returns to the planet and the employees mainly take the form of contributions to charitable causes, reduction of carbon footprint, and profit sharing and/or stock options to employees.

Suddenly, the bottom line is not so simple. Organizations have their own survival issues and profit interests, but they live in a local and global community and are increasingly waking up to (or being forced to wake up to) becoming accountable for their actions.

This change has come about for a variety of reasons: (i) the changing values among stakeholders, i.e., the notion that multiple *stake*holders — a combination of employees, managers, the larger community, and the environment itself — define the organization, not just *stock*holders; (ii) the employees' desire for an organization of which they can be proud; and (iii) the shift in values of the CEOs, which has partly come about because of personal internal contradictions, such as heart attacks, cancer, and other lifestyle diseases, as well as external pressures, such as looking out their windows and seeing angry protesters (sometimes their own children).

This growing awareness and humane mindset clarifies our purchasing power and makes it possible to "vote with our dollar" in ways undreamed of prior to the rise of the conscious consumer. Like all that came before, conscious consumerism is a step on the ladder of our collective evolution. In another ten years or so, we may see the rise of the "sacred consumer," but that's another story.

In the process of manifestation or creation, there are three main steps: the **Why** (the intention or purpose), the **How** (the means), and the **What** (the result or bottom line).

For hundreds of years, the concept of the bottom line in business has been synonymous with money earned, markets controlled, or power over the competition. In other words, the *What* was given first order of priority at the expense of the *How* and the *Why,* leaving the end to justify the means and dictate the purpose. Pioneered by the human potential movement and evolved and embraced by green and sustainable businesses, the new paradigm dethrones the absolute authority of money and measures success in broader terms. The top-down, vertical, patriarchal hierarchy has been exchanged for a horizontal, conscious business model.

This model is concerned with the means, adding the Second and Third Bottom Lines — or *How* we run our business. Important were matters of self-esteem, integrity, trust, character, and caring for the earth and the environment. Awareness and consciousness entered the picture.

Evolving these principles even further, Sacred Commerce expands the meaning of profit by introducing the concept and the reality of the *Fourth Bottom Line*, which becomes our first and primary concern. This means the return to the spiritual Self, the part of us that is in Partnership with the Divine and in tune with the Pulse of all things.

The Fourth Bottom Line is not only the return *to* the spiritual Self, but also ushers in the return *of* the spiritual Self. You are the one you have been waiting for!

While researching the Fourth Bottom Line, I was delighted to find a link to Dr. Sohail Inayatullah, Professor at Tamkang University and Queensland University of

Technology. He also identifies "Spirituality as the Fourth Bottom Line." In an article of the same name, posted on the *Metafuture* website (*metafuture.org*), Inayatullah writes about the positive repercussions of putting this concept into practice. "Happiness thus becomes an inner measure of quality of life, moving away from the quantity of things. As nations move to postmodern economies, other issues are becoming more important, among them is the spiritual. It is ceasing to be associated with mediums or with feudal religions, but about life meaning... [and] the bliss beyond pleasure and pain."

This means keeping the scientific and mystical parts of spirituality, but not acceding to the dogmatic, the sexist, or the feudal dimensions. All traditions grow up in certain historical conditions. Once things change, we can release what is no longer needed, learn from history, and move forward. Developing our spiritual Self means neither retreating to a cave nor being subjected to marginalization or ridicule. Combining the Triple Bottom Line with spirituality as the Fourth can be a vital catalyst of change within business culture as well as within our lives.

This spiritual return to self is all about the *Why*. It is the most important step, cutting to the chase and revealing our purpose and intention. In this model, we no longer do business primarily for profit, we do it because it makes us more loving, more intimate, more caring, and happier, revealing more of who we are, our intrinsic Beauty, Goodness, and Truth; in short, a spiritual profit. The "profit" of our business becomes the greater sense of meaning in our lives, along with the satisfaction of creating a positive impact. The payout of the Fourth Bottom Line is an alignment with our destiny and a personal Partnership with the Divine.

The Fourth Bottom Line encourages us to look at our motives for doing what we do. It gives us the opportunity to see through motivations, such as "competing with my siblings," "proving to my parents that I can amount to something," "getting the approval and admiration of my peers and society," "going after the American dream," or simply "the desire to earn some money." These motives have often unconsciously determined our choice of work.

Of crucial importance to the *Why* we do what we do is the question of *How* we conduct ourselves — and this is where the practice of Sacred Commerce becomes a spiritual path. Growing awareness of our purpose or intention allows us to turn off the negative ego, fear-fueled or greed-based autopilots currently conducting business within our world. Opening our eyes and ears, as well as our intuition, we become willing to see how outdated patterns and concepts are constricting our thinking and perception.

With Sacred Commerce, we become fierce in our dedication to build genuine integrity, trust, and character every step of the way. The means — or the *How* — are all-important and they can't be sacrificed at the expense of the *What* or the Return on Investment. Actually, if placed in the sacred order of *Why, How,* and *What,* the "material" bottom line is often not only achieved, but sometimes accomplished beyond what is desired, expected, or imagined; the portal to the miraculous opens!

The initial questions asked would be simple: Why am I really doing this? How does it enrich my life? Does it make me a better person? Does it lift my Abundance to Prosperity? How does it make me more loving, more understanding, more intimate and caring? Does it make me more empathic and forgiving? Does it add to my inner peace, to my elegance and grace? How does it strengthen the quality of my relationship and Partnership with the Divine? Does it add to my joy and happiness? Does it reveal my Beauty, Goodness, and Truth?

If the activities we are doing as our work do not lead us to such rewards, there is little or no return to our spiritual self. There may well be a return in terms of money and that is good and is highly recommended. There may be a return to the community and the earth, which is great. However, in the context of Sacred Commerce, we look at the spiritual return or Fourth Bottom Line first and then simply allow the other three bottom lines to successfully unfold with ease and elegance.

Our prime directive for engaging in Sacred Commerce is this: "I am in tune with my purpose and destiny." Our choice of work is aligned with what we came here to this planet to do, putting our feet squarely on that path. Each transaction, phone call, exchange, or networking event helps us on our way back home. A feeling of confidence and enthusiasm infuses all that we do. The steps of getting there become the quality of being there. This spiritual Fourth Bottom Line is a reward no worldly success, no bank balance, no trophy, no gold medal, or award can touch. This is about soul-satisfaction and the fulfillment of our need for happiness.

The King of Bhutan, one of the pioneers of GNH or "Gross National Happiness," is providing his people with an unusual yardstick to measure their nation's wealth. Equity, good governance, and harmony with nature are what this king has in mind for the citizens of his country. Instead of the traditional GNP or "Gross National Product" that measures total value of all goods and services produced, the king wants to champion his people in terms of how happy they feel. As he guides them into the domain of democracy, his values reflect what America's founding fathers named an "inalienable right": *the pursuit of happiness.*

Many have stumbled onto this path in the natural course of their personal or spiritual development. In San Francisco, where Rowan and I met with Matthew and Terces Englehardt, the founders of *Café Gratitude,* to discuss co-creating a chain of raw food restaurants, we immediately recognized their sense of soul-satisfaction. As we sat in their restaurant enjoying our meal, the atmosphere positively sparkled with gratitude; they had clearly filled their workplace with appreciation and created their food with love. Sharing our ideas on Sacred Commerce with our new friends, we explained that they were clearly already in tune with the concept, just without the label. When they adopted the term, we felt truly honored. Since then, Terces and Matthew have come up with their own beautiful way to describe the practice: "Sacred Commerce means having 'the Eternal' present in a commercial environment, making the creation of money a sacrament and the exchange of goods and services a holy opportunity, so that *'love* is the bottom line.'"

It is quite possible that in no other time in history so many have felt this call of destiny and purpose. For millions of individuals worldwide, the spiritual Self is reawakening and being called into service and purposeful action, with people streaming in droves toward meaningful careers and endeavors. Sustainability, ecology, and raising consciousness in every aspect of our daily lives are only the beginning!

PART TWO

THE MERCHANT
PRIESTHOOD

THE MERCHANT PRIESTHOOD
____ OF THE ANCIENT WORLD ____

LONG AGO IN ANCIENT EGYPT, THE ENTIRE MEDITERRANEAN basin was dotted with temples. These shrines were more than places of worship; they were points of power on an invisible web serving as places of sanctuary for the common people. Amongst those members of the priestly caste, who had conceived and built these temples, it was understood that they comprised an intricate network of nodal points. Each temple was a vortex — a node or place of joining — that drew energy from the stars and the planets, including our Earth as well. These nodes were like a lightning rod, designed to attract cosmic energy and draw it toward the earth, where it could be put to good use. The network of temples was perfectly aligned along specific *ley lines*, which the Egyptians discerned through advanced understanding of sacred geometry and geomancy.

Sacred geometry is also known as "the architecture of the universe" or "the fingerprint of God." The various patterns and symmetry can be found in every aspect of the natural world and throughout the theologies and philosophies of the ancient world. The principles of sacred geometry are believed to be of ancient Egyptian origin, clearly visible in the harmonious proportions of their temples and buildings

— and subsequently used in the planning and construction of religious structures all over the world. The Golden Mean is the cosmic language and universal principle of all things. This Divine Proportion has been found in plants, animals skeletons, the human body, chemical compounds, and the geometry of crystals and, recently, connections have been found to the human genome, DNA.

Geomancy, from the Greek roots *geo* meaning "earth" and *manteia* meaning "divination," is the ancient practice of interpreting topographical markers, relying in large measure on intuitive pattern recognition. It is closely connected to the science of Feng Shui and also to the notion of *ley lines,* first proposed in 1921 by Alfred Watkins, when he noticed that many ancient ruins, as well as churches, hilltops, stone monuments, and castles were often found to be positioned along straight lines.

The priests and priestesses who inhabited and trained in these sacred temples lived at a very high frequency. So elevated was their personal vibration, they could access spiritual insight at will and disseminate universal intelligence to the population of the region.

Each morning at sunrise, as old Sol ascended the horizon and began to kiss the sky, a wave of solar energy would move through the temples and fan out. As the radiant warmth spread across the entire country, the people would awaken and rise to meet the day. With their circadian rhythms precisely attuned to the sun in this way, they awoke profoundly revitalized and refreshed.

The priests of ancient Egypt had vocations and roles above and beyond what we are accustomed to in our time. Back then, there were no public schools or universities; the temples were the centers of learning and the priests were the teachers, specializing in different disciplines. Some Egyptian priests never left the temple; they served by staying in perpetual dialogue with the universal current of life. Other priests were scribes, healers, teachers, mediators, and celebrants. Still others were known as the Merchant Priests, who worked with the Gift of Commerce, as a mission to serve humanity.

Whereas Healing Priests worked with people on an individual basis, the Merchant Priests focused on society as a whole, attending to the bigger picture and working to balance the collective psychic state. They traveled specific energy pathways that were known to them because of their high vibration. These energy pathways, or *ley lines*, became the trade routes that led from one temple to the next, allowing precious goods to be exchanged between regions. Turquoise, for example, would be exchanged for herbs or incense — and fine fabrics for hand-woven baskets. These items were primarily of a high-vibrational quality, prized objects and elements, the presence of which raised people's consciousness, making them feel more elated, either by the object's Beauty or its intrinsic Resonance or vibration, such as the healing vibration of precious essential oils from flowers.

Whether animal, mineral, or plant, the value of the goods lay in the fact that they were infused with spiritual power and carried the frequencies that helped maintain the balance of energy in a particular place. This was a work of extraordinary refinement. Only much later, as culture began to slide into darker times and as the balance tipped toward more chauvinistic principles, did trade devolve into the unconscious exchange of goods and services that we experience today.

Merchant Priests knew that a healthy society must have a solid foundation. Principles of flow, balance, and Abundance were understood as essential and Commerce was a key means to achieve these ends. The Merchant Priesthood assumed responsibility for assuring Abundance and allowing goods to flow freely throughout the realm to the entire population. They watched over and shepherded the ebb and flow of exchange between the different levels of society, thereby ensuring that wealth did not get bottlenecked. No one place or social class could pool resources at the expense of another.

Goods were viewed as vessels of energy and also a means to engage and connect on a personal level. Trade, in many ways, functioned as social intercourse. The Merchant Priests placed great value on cultivating empathy and friendly relationships, in order to form a basis for commercial dealings. These qualities and a general sense of conviviality fostered a balanced psychic state in individuals. Relationships were understood to be the means by which this harmonious state was established throughout a culture. In summary, the Merchant Priests knew that Emotional Intelligence was a prerequisite for Prosperity. After all, it was Prosperity rather than profit that was most important to them. Abundance is having access to resources needed at the time they are needed; Prosperity is the enjoyment and the sharing of this Abundance.

Training in the Merchant Priesthood involved many, many years of study, learning about Emotional Alchemy. This knowledge and understanding deeply infused the Priests' commercial dealings and daily lives.

Often, though not always, the Priests were recognized and chosen for the calling in their infancy. Senior Priests would tour the villages looking for children who showed signs of having been part of the Merchant Priesthood in a previous life. This is not unlike the practice in Tibet, whereby lamas look for an honored teacher to return in his next incarnation.

A senior Priest would approach a potential candidate and listen to the child's heartbeat. Then, beating a drum in that rhythm, they would watch to see if the child moved in a certain way. If the child showed physical integration and made full use of his or her lower body, it meant the child was a likely candidate. Other tests would follow, similar again to those used by the Tibetans. For example, a number of objects would be placed in the child's view, among them an object typically carried by a Merchant Priest. If the child recognized and reached for that object, it was taken as a sign. Alternatively, a leopard skin — one of the symbols of the Priesthood — would be placed on the ground amongst many other skins. If the child crawled onto the leopard skin, this was another good indication he or she had been a Merchant Priest in a former life.

This practice was also common amongst the Native American tribe of the Hopi people. When children of the tribe reached two years old, a collection of toys would be presented to them. The tribal elders would watch to see which toy became the child's favorite. The child who favored a drum or a rattle — the tools of the shaman — would be directed to a different teacher than the child who consistently played with the bow and arrow or other tools of the warrior.

In some cases, a specific body type — a shorter than average and stocky frame — was the clue that an individual was destined for the Merchant Priesthood. Given that the Merchant Priests watched over the temple treasuries, some of them had to be small enough to pass through the secret entrances, where the riches were stored.

The deity that presided over and protected the Merchant Priesthood was Bes, the god of Commerce. It is believed that Bes was originally a person who lived in Atlantis, who later became the archetypal symbol of the good things in life and the protector against evil. He is also found in the Great Lakes area of Africa, in the Congo and Rwanda and in pre-dynastic Nile Valley cultures.

Bes was initially a protector god of the Pharaoh, although his dominion grew over time to include all households, especially significant to mothers and children. It was he who presided over birth, the gateway between the spiritual and the material worlds. His portly fullness represented his alliance with midwives and his capacity to bring forth a soul to the earthly plane. For Egyptians, to greet an incoming soul with the means by which that soul could satisfy all material needs was essential — an ethical imperative that society took upon itself to fulfill. From their perspective, humans were spiritual beings coming to Earth to experiment on the physical plane — and were to be properly provisioned.

It was believed that during a birth, Bes would dance about the room, shaking his rattle to ensure the baby's safe passage from the spirit world to the earthly plane. Should a problem arise during labor or delivery, a statue of Bes would be placed on the mother's head and the dwarf god was called on for help. Later, should an infant begin to laugh or giggle without apparent cause, it was believed that Bes was nearby, making funny faces at the little one.

Like the laughing Buddha, Bes was the god of laughter and joy, often represented with his tongue sticking out. His earthly joy was transformative; through laughter, he transmuted the so-called constricting energies of fear, anger, and jealousy into their higher frequencies of compassion, passion, and grace.

The god Bes also played a key role in chasing away evil spirits and demons; households would often keep a statue of him, standing near the door. Since he was able to drive away evil, Bes became associated with all the good things in life: music, dance, and all forms of pleasure.

During the period from approximately 332 to 30 BC, the Greek period in ancient Egypt, images of Bes proliferated in the form of amulets, figurines, and full-scale reliefs in temples such as Dendera and Abydos, elevating Bes to the Egyptian Pantheon, alongside the great gods. He eventually made his way overseas and was popular among the Phoenicians and the people of Cyprus. Many believe that the god Bes was Christianized by the Italians in the cult of St. Bessus, who is also invoked for fertility. When Phoenician settlers made their way to one of the Balearic Islands, where no venomous creatures lived, they were convinced it was the island of Bes and some believe this is how the island of Ibiza got its name. There is also a connection between Bes and the Celtic "green man," again a symbol of fertility — and also with the gargoyles on churches and cathedrals, used to ward off evil.

INITIATION
AND TRAINING

EMOTIONAL ALCHEMY WAS THE PRIMARY FOCUS OF Merchant Priesthood training. This involved a deep education that spanned years, if not decades, and led to a profound understanding of the lower centers — or lower Chakras — and the associated root emotions. Once initiated on the path, the Merchant Priest-in-training began to explore and develop the *hara* — the vital center below the navel that is the seat of emotional power.

As we've mentioned, both men and women alike were called to follow the path of the Merchant Priesthood and the training was first and foremost the study and mastery of the emotional realm. While both genders trained rigorously and engaged in similar activities, the male Priests were more engaged in trading activities and traveled extensively, while the Priestesses were more responsible for maintaining a high vibration — or Resonance. The women did this by entering a meditative state and expanding their awareness to a point where they were literally responsible for crafting the collective emotional sphere of a gathering or the Resonance within a temple. They became very still inside and, once this was achieved, they called in specific Resonances, drawing forward the eternal verities of Beauty, Goodness, and Truth.

For the Merchant Priestess, this form of meditation was a process of both inner and outer refinement.

As part of this early training, acolytes — often children — were brought to the marketplace, so that they could witness and grow accustomed to the intense, ever-shifting, emotional environment surrounding trade negotiations. Learning to recognize and "read" emotions in fine detail, they attended to many different layers and levels of expression.

From physical manifestations such as muscle tension, skin tone, vocal quality, facial expression, and even heart rate and blood pressure, the Merchant Priest learned to sense the texture and temperature of the emotional side of trade. In time, they developed the ability to equalize and balance the energy of emotions that swirled around the marketplace.

Imagine for a moment, a Zen master walking around the stock market in the heat of a trading day, while brokers and traders clamor all around him. This is the depth of presence and awareness the Merchant Priests carried with them when they walked through the markets. In addition, they knew how to shift the clamoring into a higher order of exchange or Resonance.

This then, was the Merchant Priests' ministry: raising the frequency/vibration of an emotion, whereby the emotion is lifted or raised from a lower octave to a higher one, such as, for example, lifting the root emotion of fear to a level where it could be felt as concern. Fear tends to cause a person to choose between the "flight," "fight," or "freeze" response, whereas concern arouses compassion, which in turn leads to action. Likewise, a Merchant Priest could also transform the root emotion of anger into courage, courage into passion, and so on.

Humanity had very little emotional maturity at the time when the Merchant Priesthood was most active. In fact, the general public was largely illiterate when it came to emotions. The marketplace was rife with envy, jealousy, anger, and even outright rage. The Merchant Priests would literally "minister" to the collective psychic state, by going to the marketplace, sitting out of the way, and closing their eyes in meditation. With their vast capacity for empathy, they would draw all the negativity into their own bodies and then, using their bodies and minds as alchemical chambers, they would transform these raw emotions into compassion, passion, and empathy. The Priests would then breathe these refined emotional frequencies back out into the marketplace, infusing the shared psychic space with a higher, more balanced emotional tone. (This will be fully explained later in the book; and practices shared so you can begin develop these skills yourself.)

Learning how to recognize and respond to the root emotions was an essential part of the Merchant Priests' training. They were taught, for example, how to recognize and contain the emotion of jealousy. Jealousy is called "the green-eyed monster" for good reason and, along with anger and fear, can be one of the most troublesome human emotions because of the passion it evokes. Merchant Priests were highly sensitized to jealousy, learning first to experience it fully in themselves. Tending to emotion in a literate and intelligent way, individuals learned to *listen* to what "the green-eyed monster" had to say, seeing it as an ally. By respecting the emotion as a communication containing vital information, they would listen to its signal and learn about what they truly wanted, lifting it to a state of grace — the ability to receive what is truly theirs.

The more the Merchant Priests were able to contain their own life energies in this way, the more they were able to feel the emotions of others and manage the collective psychic state for the greater good, without anyone ever knowing what they were doing. With training, the Merchant Priests became masters of this process. In a sense, they were the first real diplomats, as theirs was the work of negotiation. Humanity had so little emotional maturity that the intervention and ministry of the Merchant Priesthood was essential to the emotional sphere of their society. Not until a level of emotional maturity began to percolate into people's minds and hearts did the concept of negotiation become accessible. Until that time, it was the responsibility of the Merchant Priests. They could literally assist and, in a sense, "sculpt" the emotional Resonance of the marketplace. Some were so skillful, they would simply resonate with the higher aspect of a particular emotion, radiating it outward to counteract any base feelings before they could take hold. This was the Merchant Priests' unique science and area of expertise.

Managing the lower centers or lower Chakras in this way was not limited to the sphere of business. The Merchant Priests also stayed in touch with and maintained balance in the general psychic tone of the culture and were responsible for more practical things, like reading the *Nilometer*, a device designed to monitor the rise and fall of the river Nile.

Thanks to the work of the Merchant Priests, the Egyptians had a harmonious relationship with the Nile. The great river was essential to their livelihood and to the growth of agriculture — and in addition, was a primary line of communication. It was the lifeline that fed travel, transportation, and trade, as essential then as satellites are to us today. The Nilometer warned when floods were coming and helped foresee whether they would be high or low, early or late. With a deep appreciation for the forces of nature and astronomy, the Merchant Priests understood that the floods made the land fertile and added to their overall Abundance.

Upon reading the Nilometer, the Priests would issue instructions about the ideal crops and the best times for planting them. If an irregular flood pattern interrupted a planting season, the Priests would sense this and stabilize the fear and anxiety that could potentially spread throughout the collective.

The Priests were also trained to read psychic changes that occurred with the cycles of the moon; lunar influences on both individuals and the collective were noted and addressed. The ancient Egyptians had a highly developed psychic ability, but they were also deeply embodied and grounded in the practical world. It was this balance between the emphasis and value placed on psychic sensitivity and the grounded practical abilities that allowed the Merchant Priests to become one of the most respected of the priestly castes.

Their sensitivity to the subtleties of psychic irregularities explains why the leopard became their symbol. Like the sleek cat whose nighttime stealth is legendary, Merchant Priests were masters at reading both individual people and the collective psyche, able to see into the depths of the human subconscious. In today's world, this ability has been reduced to certain groups of mediums and psychics or degraded and placed in the hands of the tabloids. In Egypt, the Priests — not the paparazzi — oversaw the dark side. They could sense negative energies the moment they began to emerge and transmute them before external damage occurred.

The Egyptians understood that a healthy society relied on the unique contribution of every part. The Healer Priests, for example, experienced an extraordinary degree of compassion, which earned them deep love and respect not only from the general public, but also from the other priestly castes. Although Merchant Priests were also trained to develop compassion, the Healer Priests were the ones who fully mastered this quality.

Following his theory of the three elements of the soul, the ancient Greek philosopher Plato, writing about Egypt, divided ancient Egyptian society into three classes: craftsmen, soldiers, and philosophers. The craftsmen represented the digestive forces; they digested the food of the gods, the raw material of the earth, which, in turn, became art or **Beauty**. The soldiers represented the heart; they mastered the three emotions that reside within the heart: love, joy, and sorrow. The greatest soldiers were those who had been baptized by love, because they had something to fight for that was true — the frequency of **Goodness**. Before going into battle, soldiers would seek the blessing of the lion goddess, Sekhmet. Their hearts would thus be cleansed of all conflict, allowing them to concentrate and focus the mind with single-pointed purpose on the matter at hand. Finally, the philosophers or guardians represented the head or **Truth**, holding the needs and the interests of society above their own. These three parts worked together as a seamless, organic whole.

Comparatively speaking, the Merchant Priesthood was like a postdoctorate level of training. Its members were trained and tested, and conducted deep personal research into the psychic and practical functioning of all three levels of society. These men and women expressed their love through their concern for the bigger picture — the overall welfare of the people and their environment, rather than personal love — keeping a keen eye on the whole. Functionally, their main job was like that of Plato's craftsmen. At the same time, they infused all commercial undertakings with genuine empathy and intuitive sensitivity, which acted as both a lubricant and a shock absorber, allowing everything to flow and run smoothly.

ORIGINS, LEGEND,
_____ AND MYTH _____

LEGEND TELLS THAT THE MERCHANT PRIESTHOOD THRIVED —
and may well have originated — in the now mythical
land known as Atlantis. When that civilization disappeared
beneath the waves, it is believed that a few survivors escaped
and remnants of the culture resurfaced in Egypt and many
other parts of the world. Legend talks about Isis and Osiris
landing in Egypt and bringing with them the sacred teachings and knowledge of the Merchant Priesthood.

Historically, we see the first real signs of the Merchant
Priesthood during Queen Hatshepsut's reign from 1479 to
1458 BC. Known as the era of the "New Kingdom," this
period saw Egypt develop into a great empire, as wealth
and new ideas spread across the country. By the time
Queen Hatshepsut began her reign, officials were already
being selected on merit instead of the more traditional
system, whereby authority was passed through family lines
and inheritance. This strongly suggests the influence of the
Merchant Priests, who — by their own nature and the
nature of their work — were predisposed to protecting
meritocratic principles.

Old Egypt was a center for learning, art, and culture;
it was a place where people came to learn who they were

as human beings — beings of light, emotions, and energy. However, at the time of Queen Hatshepsut's reign, huge amounts of wealth were being squandered on their military forces and defending boundaries.

When the queen declared herself the transitory leader of Egypt, her central goal was to restore the principles of celebration, as advocated by the goddess Hathor, the deity of joy, Beauty, feminine love, and music. She fully understood the concept of "adding one drop of joy to transform oceans of fear, anger, and jealousy." By creating festivals for Hathor, the queen magically transformed Egypt's relationship with her neighbors, from one of war to one of peace.

The Temple Complex of Dendera celebrated both the goddess Hathor and Bes, the god of the Merchant Priesthood. A huge mural is carved on the wall of Hathor's funerary temple, which is unique in Egypt and in history. It depicts scenes from Queen Hatshepsut's reign, her reopening of the old trade routes, and various trade guilds bringing offerings to their queen.

These guilds are another indication of the presence of the Merchant Priesthood. Queen Hatshepsut encouraged and supported their role among the priestly caste, raising them to the highest office and esteem during her reign. At her bequest, the Merchant Priests opened the trade routes to encourage commerce with other cultures. The route between Egypt and the Land of Punt, which is located near present-day Somalia, was opened during this time. The Merchant Priests served their benevolent queen well and this new trade route allowed her subjects to enjoy highly prized imports, such as spices, gold, and aromatic plants.

Simultaneously, these activities began to bring different cultures and communities together to learn from each other.

Unlike statues or murals depicting other Egyptian pharaohs, paintings of Hatshepsut show the Merchant Priests standing tall rather than bowing in the presence of their queen. This shows strongly the esteem she had for them — and they for her — and suggests the democratic principle of equality was valued during her reign.

Although Egypt was then in a position to reconquer many surrounding territories, the queen chose to use Commerce as a link to the well-being of not only her own country and citizens, but also that of her neighbors. By establishing trade links with them, she simultaneously made peace, whereby they all prospered together.

The Merchant Priests were esteemed during Hatshepsut's reign and the people enjoyed Abundance as a result. Sadly, Hatshepsut's successor, Thutmose III, undid nearly all the progress his stepmother had made during her twenty-year rule. Favoring war over trade, he displaced the Merchant Priests and stripped them of almost all of their authority and influence.

This is typical of the history of the Merchant Priesthood and their successors, rising when the feminine and sacred values emerge within a culture and subsequently going underground beneath the next wave of chauvinistic, authoritarian, and patriarchal principles. Concerned for their lives, the Merchant Priests formed secret societies, protecting themselves and concealing their activities from the ruling classes.

When the Merchant Priests were demoted by Thutmose III, the delicate social and psychic balance began to wobble, opening the way for him to make war. Instead of trading goods and sharing culture, he began a mission to vanquish and plunder Egypt's former trade partners.

A war economy tends to give the temporary illusion of wealth and, indeed, Egypt seemed to prosper under the reign of Thutmose III. Yet he nearly bankrupted the country. However, the remnants of the Merchant Priesthood managed to stave off complete economic collapse, by conspiring to support the next pharaoh, Thutmose IV.

The new pharaoh was aware that the Giza complex had always been the core energy source of Egypt. Known in modern times as one of the Seven Wonders of the Ancient World, the pyramids at Giza are the most majestic necropolis — or cemetery — known to mankind. The complex is comprised of the Great Pyramid, the smaller Pyramid of Khafre, the smaller still Pyramid of Menkaure, a number of satellite pyramids of the queens, causeways and valley pyramids, as well as the stunning Great Sphinx.

In a vision, Thutmose IV saw that if the complex could once again be sparked into life, it had the power to restabilize and energize the entire country. With this knowledge, he went on to rebuild the country's infrastructure and in so doing, he reinstated many of the displaced Merchant Priests. During his reign, Egypt once again prospered.

Legend tells of the Merchant Priesthood designing an initiatory encounter for Thutmose IV involving the Sphinx. The site had been barred during the previous pharaoh's reign, because it had been such a powerful vortex for initiations. When Thutmose IV came into power, the Merchant Priests arranged for the new ruler to sleep between the Sphinx's paws. A kind of giant cosmic tuning fork, the paws created a high frequency energy field. While sleeping in this most sacred of sacred spots, the pharaoh had a revelation followed by vision after vision of various civil projects that would revitalize the Giza complex and the Sphinx itself. These civil projects in turn revived an economy that had become depleted and crippled by years of war.

Within the reign of another pharaoh, Akhenaten, the reach and influence of the Merchant Priests once again expanded after having gone again into the background again during the thirty-year reign of Amenhotep III. They were given responsibility for myriad construction projects from temple restoration to the building of an entirely new capital city.

Akhenaten was a great champion and leader of the Merchant Priesthood and a revolutionary in many ways. Some of the most essential features of the Merchant Priesthood's vision of a healthy society were ushered to the fore during Akhenaten's reign. People openly worshiped Ra, as the One God, a practice that had formerly been limited to a hidden mystery cult. Although it was his father, Amenhotep III, who had initiated the movement toward monotheism — going so far as to proclaim his young son "the Messiah" — it was really Akhenaten who spearheaded monotheism by bringing worship of Ra out into the open.

In the course of advancing this new form of religion, Akhenaten liberated Egyptian art from rigidly stylized forms. Statues of Akhenaten and his wife, Queen Nefertiti, look strangely modern. As works of art, they almost appear to be cousins of much later works by Modigliani and Rodin. He also allowed the Merchant Priests to bring artists from the island of Crete to Egypt. Minoan art introduced a different style and a new way of looking at the world that was less encumbered by an exaggerated belief that all rewards lay in the afterlife.

At that point in Cretan history, civilization was centered around celebration and investing oneself in the joys of the here-and-now. The life of the senses was highly valued, not as hedonistic indulgence, but as a soulful celebration of the spirit in matter. Throughout their entire history, one of the sacred purposes of the Merchant Priesthood has been to unite spirit and matter.

Akhenaten fostered the vision of a non-violent, almost democratic society and his reign saw the first flowering of a rational philosophy, as well as the bare beginnings of a school of scientific thought. Akhenaten even dreamed of a single civilization throughout the Mediterranean, united by a complex web of trade routes and free trade among all peoples — one of the first seeds of what we now talk of as "the Globalization Movement."

Akhenaten was a revolutionary in another sense as well; some consider him to have foreshadowed feminism. Unlike other sovereigns of his time, his wife was an equal, ruling side by side with him.

In essence, Akhenaten brought the feminine back and opened the door to the everyday sacred. Oddly enough, this was also his Achilles' heel. Akhenaten and Nefertiti were both so focused, some say obsessed, with steering Egypt back onto a spiritual track that they tended to ignore certain very real threats. Hostile neighbors, intent on military invasion and intrigues against the pharaoh by the priests of Thebes, began to loom large. These negative energies grew in force. However, the pharaoh and his wife existed in such a high vibration, they could barely keep themselves in their bodies. The art they left behind has led some to surmise that they went so far in their process of merging spirit and matter that for them, matter itself nearly dematerialized.

Akhenaten was the last pharaoh to revere Joseph, the Hebrew with the many-colored coat. An early Merchant Priest, Joseph had lived in Egypt hundreds of years before Akhenaten.

You may recall the story of Joseph being sold into slavery in Egypt by his brothers, after he told them of his dream. In his sleep, Joseph saw a sheaf of corn standing upright in a circle of eleven sheaves. All the other sheaves were bowing to the one in the middle; the honored sheaf was Joseph. Exacerbated by the fact that their father, Jacob, had always favored Joseph, his youngest son, this dream image got the better of the brothers and they secretly sold their baby brother into slavery.

Once in Egypt, however, Joseph did not remain a slave for long. Word of him as a gifted interpreter of dreams reached the pharaoh, who'd experienced a troubling series of dreams, which his advisors could not help him to understand. Joseph was called in to discuss the pharaoh's dreams of seven fat cows, followed by seven lean cows that ate the fat ones.

Joseph interpreted the dream as prophetic, indicating that the cows were a symbolic prediction of seven prosperous years of good harvests followed by seven lean ones, characterized by famine and drought. Joseph recommended the pharaoh make wise use of the resources gathered in the years of plenty, storing them in granaries: sustainability in its earliest form. The pharaoh took his advice, commissioning

Joseph to build the granaries and, sure enough, after the years of good harvest, the famine came. During these lean years, Egypt was the only country in the whole region with grain, the measure and standard of wealth at that time. The pharaoh rewarded Joseph by promoting him to a position of leadership, as the head of the Merchant Priesthood. In ancient Egyptian, the word "Joseph," came to mean "Master of the Granaries."

Joseph also championed the use of the Nilometer. With it, he was able to foresee whether the Nile flood would be high or low and could advise the people on what to plant and where. While other agrarian societies in the region suffered, Egypt fared well.

During the seven long years of famine, Joseph's father and brothers came to Egypt in search of grain, approaching the "Master of the Granaries" on bended knee and begging for food. He didn't reveal his identity right away, but gave his family all they needed, expressing stern compassion, as well as generosity.

Among the many hidden morals in this tale is an important layer of meaning that can help us understand the influence of the Merchant Priests. As we have seen, the Merchant Priests always stood for the protection of the democratic process. In the ascent of the youngest brother, the story questions the accepted traditional social hierarchy within the family; the social system at the time of Joseph sought to uphold patriarchal authority by passing it down through the eldest male.

The story shows us that life has its own intelligent process and will gather whatever forces are needed to manifest its inherent patterns. Those patterns are seeds or archetypes that have been there from the beginning. One such pattern is the tendency of organisms to move toward an egalitarian system of flow — the flow of energy in all its different forms and directions. This is what we really mean by democracy; a system that allows optimum energy flow, rather than a hierarchal system where energy becomes blocked or locked up in privileged compartments.

As the story goes, Jacob and his sons stayed in Egypt, where, over time, the Hebrews became an honored people. Many Hebrews were trained in the Merchant Priesthood and their contribution and involvement in Commerce can be traced back to this time.

By the time Akhenaten took the throne many decades later, however, conflict between the Hebrews and Egyptians had begun to stir. His reign was peppered with conflict from the start, largely because of his allegiance and loyalty to his non-Egyptian mother, Queen Tiye.

In addition, the high priests in the capital city, Thebes, objected to the god Ra being raised above all others, because this reduced their power as clergy of the polytheistic religion. Faced with assassination threats, Akhenaten left Thebes, traveling north along the Nile, where, on virgin ground, he built an entirely new city.

Legend suggests that a number of Theban priests had conceived a plot to assassinate Akhenaten, devising a plan to take possession of his corpse. They intended to use their magic arts to tap into Akhenaten's memory banks and distort the esoteric knowledge pertaining to the One God he had received from his father. However, Akhenaten's disappearance foiled their plan. Legend has it that he and his wife dematerialized, transmuting themselves into pure light.

Following Akhenaten's disappearance, the Theban priests led Egypt back to polytheism, obliterating every trace of the pharaoh's name. However, the seed of a monotheistic vision, as well as the seeds of the Merchant Priesthood, had been planted amongst the Hebrews and it quietly began to grow.

Before Akhenaten disappeared, it is believed he initiated one of his advisors in the northern city into the full mysteries of monotheistic religion. This is the man we know as Moses. This is how Moses came to embody the knowledge and vision of Akhenaten, as both a High Priest of the prevailing Egyptian rites and an advisor in a northern city.

In addition to introducing him to the notion of One God, Akhenaten shared with him the secrets of the Merchant Priesthood. It is likely that Moses passed the esoteric knowledge down through other highly placed Hebrews, while handing over to the people a set of simple behavioral guidelines known as the Ten Commandments. The Hebrew people were thus endowed with both the means and the structure for a whole new stage of growth and development.

We muse that the secret scrolls, taken from Egypt by Moses and associated with the Ark of the Covenant, may well have contained a master plan for a balanced society that had at its core the practice of Sacred Commerce and Emotional Alchemy.

The reason Moses led the Hebrews out of Egypt was to free them from slavery. Rameses had been unable to contain his jealousy and felt the Hebrews had become too prosperous. Their growing numbers and wealth made him nervous, so he enslaved them. Previously, Egypt had been a multicultural society, where many different ethnic groups flourished and moved freely across its unguarded borders. However,

Rameses stopped the flow of free trade and tried to centralize power, holding it exclusively for himself and his chosen priests. Many Merchant Priests were sent to remote regions of the country, where their influence would be minimal, while those of Hebrew descent were enslaved.

Moses, highly skilled in the art of empathy and Emotional Alchemy, was able to unleash the plagues on Egypt by redirecting Rameses' personal emotions and projecting them back onto the collective. In ancient Egypt, the pharaoh *was* Egypt. In this case, to use the language of the Bible, "the pharaoh's heart was unusually hard." Finally, Rameses was forced to let the Hebrew people go on their way.

The point of this history is to provide a context for where we are today. What we see — and who we are now — is built on the myriad of societies that came before, honed by the process of evolution. History is one long journey of refinement and we are the ones, both as individuals and as a collective, who continue to be refined. We believe evolution's trajectory is the harmonious coexistence of all humans with the earth and all living species.

Eventually, Solomon, a descendent of Moses, built a temple in Jerusalem, much of it financed by the gold the Hebrews had carried out of Egypt. Solomon, with his principles of fairness and justice for all and not just the privileged, was the true inheritor of Moses' and the Merchant Priesthood's lineage. It was he who conducted the sacred rites that activated the Ark of the Covenant.

From the land of the Israelites, Merchant Priests and the principles of the Merchant Priesthood continued to spread across the eastern Mediterranean into Greece, where they were instrumental in the founding of many great city-states, among them Thebes, named after Akhenaten's capital in Egypt.

Several hundred years later, when Alexander invaded Egypt, the Greeks built a completely new capital city on the very site where Akhenaten's capital city had stood. They named their new city Hermopolis (later renamed Alexandria), in honor of the god Hermes. Known as the messenger god, Hermes was also the god of Commerce, communication, writing, transport, and all forms of exchange, equivalent to the god Bes in Egypt.

What we are suggesting is that it is possible to trace an unbroken line of senior Merchant Priests at least from Queen Hatshepsut down through Moses to the founding of the cradles of democracy in the city-states of Greece and beyond.

The Merchant Priesthood, through its Greek influence, was instrumental in the founding of the European world, including introducing the concept of democracy and, in around 700 BC, the creation of the first coins in Lydia, a seafaring neighboring state of the Greeks. These new coins replaced the metal rings used by the Egyptians as rudimentary coinage. It was not until the Greek civilization emerged that coinage became a fully-fledged instrument of trade and exchange. A great dream originating with Akhenaten, the invention of the coin vastly facilitated trade and interaction between all the peoples of the Mediterranean.

The work of the Merchant Priests was not limited to the Middle East, however. In the Far East, a related set of underlying Merchant Priest values also began to spread. Let us consider Lao Tzu (Laozi), for example, the great sage of Chinese Taoism, who introduced the notion of "inner ecology." Also called Feng Shui, this extensive and detailed practice involves the relationship between emotional life and geomantic energy flows. Because of Lao Tzu's Taoist influence, Chinese cities were organized in such a way as to facilitate the harmonization of the emotional life of the populace. Monks held and fulfilled responsibilities much like those assumed by the Merchant Priests in Egypt. Lao Tzu essentially united the urban social structures with the larger overall ecology.

A little-known fact is that the Egyptians practiced a kind of emotional Feng Shui, similar to our modern understanding, where each area of the house represented a part of the *bagua*, the Feng Shui blueprint. In today's *bagua*, each section of the house represents the key elements of our lives, such as our "Abundance" and "relationships." In Egyptian Feng Shui, these areas were more related to the emotions.

In Lao Tzu's time, some two and a half thousand years ago, the flow of ideas and goods was unimpeded, due to the harmonious emotional state of the country. The culture was deeply aligned with the natural energy flows of the earth and these became the trade routes, later known as the famous Silk Road.

Fifteen hundred years after Lao Tzu's time, the Chinese version of the Merchant Priests, or "commerce adventurers," invented paper money. By exciting the authorities into printing paper money, they passed the knowledge of the earliest type of printing press on to Marco Polo and Europe. With this development and the ensuing spread of literacy, the monopoly on knowledge was broken and education was no longer the exclusive privilege of the elite. This continued the process of leveling the playing field, lifting another roadblock toward democracy.

PART THREE

THE INFLUENCE OF THE
MERCHANT PRIESTHOOD

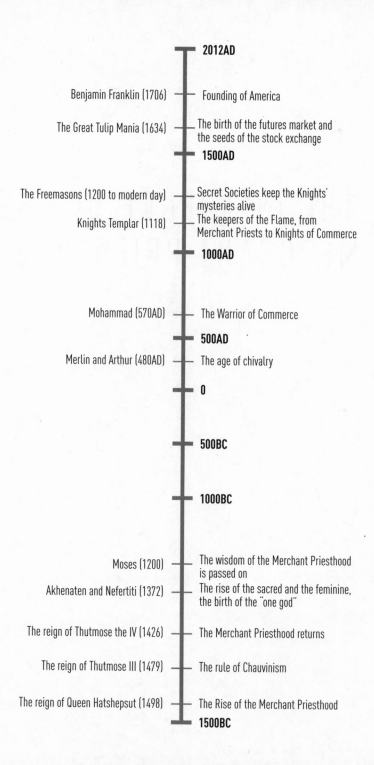

2012AD

Benjamin Franklin (1706) — Founding of America

The Great Tulip Mania (1634) — The birth of the futures market and the seeds of the stock exchange

1500AD

The Freemasons (1200 to modern day) — Secret Societies keep the Knights' mysteries alive

Knights Templar (1118) — The keepers of the Flame, from Merchant Priests to Knights of Commerce

1000AD

Mohammad (570AD) — The Warrior of Commerce

500AD

Merlin and Arthur (480AD) — The age of chivalry

0

500BC

1000BC

Moses (1200) — The wisdom of the Merchant Priesthood is passed on

Akhenaten and Nefertiti (1372) — The rise of the sacred and the feminine, the birth of the "one god"

The reign of Thutmose the IV (1426) — The Merchant Priesthood returns

The reign of Thutmose III (1479) — The rule of Chauvinism

The reign of Queen Hatshepsut (1498) — The Rise of the Merchant Priesthood

1500BC

THE MERLIN AND ARTHUR LEGACY: TO EUROPE AND THE KING'S COURT

THE CONCERN FOR ATTUNEMENT WITH NATURE EVIDENCED among the Chinese and Egyptians also lies at the heart of the tales of King Arthur. It can even be argued that Arthur and Merlin were the greatest Merchant Priests alive during a time of intense activity on the part of the Priesthood.

It is interesting to note that the Arthurian legend is an odd mixture of time frames and metaphors, leading into and from the tale of Camelot. The legendary figure, King Arthur, reigned during the late fifth to early sixth century, but the Arthurian fables of the Round Table and the Holy Grail emerged hundreds of years after the fact, embellished by and mixed with tales of chivalry and knights.

It is important to see that legends are allegories that reveal the workings of the human mind and of a man's relationship to his community. For this reason, tales like Camelot carry deep truths, which need deciphering in order for their full impact to deliver an essential understanding of human nature. Stories and parables have been used throughout time by the priestly castes for just this purpose — the dissemination of knowledge. Myths are a transmission of archetypal energy and soul wisdom, designed to nourish the spirit and help us grow in an ethical direction. In light of this, the question becomes: How do we best interpret the Arthurian legends in relation to the Merchant Priests' perspective?

Above all things, Merlin wished a good king for England and, seeing Arthur's potential, he took the boy under his wing, teaching him about chivalry. Over the following years, Merlin and Arthur envisioned and promoted the concept of chivalry as a sacred map for people to follow, with the goal of spreading goodness throughout the kingdom. Along with the Knights of the Round Table, the map was successfully promoted and spread throughout Europe, later inspiring the Knights Templar, who dedicated themselves to the principles of Beauty, Goodness, and Truth.

Each knight at the Round Table not only represented a different family and hierarchy, he represented a *specific temperament* on the spectrum of the human psyche. Accordingly, each was perceived as being suited to a particular task to which he was assigned. Furthermore, each knight was given an equal place at the Round Table, in alignment with the Merchant Priests' core principle of equality. This didn't mean that everyone or everything must be the same, rather that the playing field was leveled, where all beings and things have their proper place in relation to the whole, appreciated for what they uniquely contribute.

The Merchant Priesthood championed a view of the whole that recognized the unique value of each and every member of society. Each person of every class was to be accorded due respect and an appropriate share of the overall prosperity of the culture.

By extension, the Merchant Priests saw every emotion as having its rightful place within the overall ecology of both the individual and society as a whole. Metaphorically, the Round Table and the diverse characters seated around it were a complete map of the psychic states necessary for the proper functioning of the kingdom. Symbolically, the "kingdom" can be interpreted as either the society or the individual.

The urban court and indeed all individuals were likewise viewed from this framework. The fulfillment by every knight of his particular duty resulted in a general integration across all the emotions and, therefore, peace reigned in the kingdom.

Under these conditions of integration, everyone could enjoy the natural flow of knowledge and resources between the different segments of society and across other cultures. This was the map represented by Camelot, a symbol of where heaven comes to earth and the Beauty of the natural order is replicated in everyone.

A number of esoteric and mystical teachings point out that the Knights also represent the potential for the natural order to be replicated in a single human being. This teaching sees the Knights as symbolic of personality types, also corresponding to the signs on the zodiac.

Our favorite interpretation is the map of chivalry offered by our friend, Lazaris, who sees each knight as the embodiment of a specific quality: honor, loyalty, nobility, virtue, grace, trust, courage, courtesy, gallantry, authority, service, and humility. When all twelve qualities exist within an individual being or organization, their frequencies combine and coalesce. These twelve qualities come together to create a

Resonance called chivalry — or as we call it, Goodness. Seen from this perspective, the Knights of the Round Table are an invitation to embody the full spectrum of our Goodness in its most noble form.

The role of the female in this development is paramount, as it is the women who trigger and inspire chivalry in the men, hence the designation of women as the "Ladies of the Round." They were not necessarily the Knights' wives or lovers; most likely they were friends, sisters, or other female counterpart.

Each of the Ladies of the Round learned to attune herself to the subtle frequencies of her respective Knight's unique quality — her role being of equal importance as any man's within the sphere of the Round Table. Their collective responsibility was to hold the Resonance of those frequencies, not unlike the ministry of the Merchant Priestesses in the temples in old Egypt when they called on the Resonance of Beauty, Goodness, and Truth.

Where does the Grail come into this story? Legend finds the Knights of the Round Table searching for this mystical "vessel," a cup or an urn in which the blood of the crucified Christ had purportedly been caught. However, it is our belief that the Grail never really belonged to the dimension of earthy reality; rather it was a supreme symbol of the spiritualization of matter. In essence, the Grail represents the healing of the Immaculate Heart, the heart of Christ and the heart of the whole Christian story.

The Knights of the Round Table could only become truly united by the acquisition of the Grail. In other words, humanity can only become truly united in the radiance of love. Love is the deepest essence of our emotional being; it rules all the other emotions. At heart, love was the whole purpose of the quest, symbolized by the vision of the Holy Grail. Wherever the Grail appeared — and credible appearances occurred in extremely diverse locations — it sparked intense desire on the part of its seekers.

Reports of the Grail being seen in many places across both Britain and on the continent were common, with various churches laying claim to having the chalice at different times, none of which were proven to be fraudulent. The search for the Grail was a most challenging quest, with the inability to acquire it making it all the more venerated and ever more inspiring to its seekers. Accordingly, the Grail generated huge flows of pilgrims across Europe, which of course meant a renewed flow and exchange of ideas, culture, knowledge, and Commerce.

This marked the beginning of what we now know as "tourism." The Knights Templar, whose role in this story we will soon be exploring, encouraged pilgrimages to sacred sites, protecting the pilgrims along their way. Such journeys created trade and allowed for the exchange of culture. Again, the aim of Commerce was not simply business for business' sake. The main responsibility of the Knights Templar was to stimulate the exchange of energy, goods, and services and to connect people, so that they could appreciate and enjoy the Beauty and the wonder of each other.

Tourism and travel are fantastic tools of commerce, helping to connect people around the world, creating revenue streams, and spreading the wealth. Perhaps the Merchant Priests encouraged and fed people's fascination with the Holy Grail by intentionally moving the rumors about its location around Europe, much as the Olympic Committee moves the flaming torch around the world today.

Witness the great celebration in a city, when it is awarded the Olympic Games. Not only is it a great honor to host top athletes from around the world, but also the flood of tourists and money that follow the Olympics is a great boom to the local economy. Meanwhile, the whole world *party-cipates*, by visiting the host city or gathering in the millions in front of their television sets.

Let us return to the time of King Arthur and Merlin. Legend tells of Merlin's tutelage under Saint Kevin of Ireland. During the Dark Ages, Saint Kevin did all he could to keep breathing life into a dying civilization. With Europe in chaos after the fall of the Roman Empire, the Celts in Ireland were the continent's lifeline to civilization and the sole store of knowledge. Many Merchant Priests were born among the Irish at that time. When the Romans left, following a series of failed harvests and a variety of events on the continent, the Merchant Priests began their work in earnest.

Their first task was to restore the use of lunar and solar calendars, knowing this knowledge could help steer the population in the right direction — toward a life in harmony with the planetary cycles and energy flows. With the help of the calendars, the knowledge of what, when, and where to plant crops and how to avert famine was restored.

It was in Ireland with Saint Kevin that Merlin was given his first vision of the true meaning of the Holy Grail, seeding society with a mythology that still vibrates in our hearts today. The phenomenon surrounding Dan Brown's *The DaVinci Code* was fueled by the burning desire to finally capture and claim the secrets of the Holy Grail. After all these years and all this searching, still the relic has eluded our efforts to acquire it and hold it up for all humanity to see. Dan Brown owes much of the success of his book to this odd conundrum and even more to Merlin, one of history's most influential Merchant Priests.

No doubt we will continue to see ever more stories and spins on the theme of the Holy Grail. Humans have an insatiable appetite for truth and the Grail is one of our strongest images for that which rests at our very core: the Immaculate Heart of Love.

Merlin knew that Britain, being an island, had unique potential to develop a culture that could emerge on the world stage as the bastion of the Merchant Priests' ideology. This is why so much energy was given to the myth of the Holy Grail as a spiritual current and a tool to advance the quality of chivalry — or Goodness — in the community during the Middle Ages.

The power of myth to shape the hearts and minds of men was well understood by the Merchant Priests. The tales of King Arthur are a true example of how myth is employed to infuse culture and history with stories and legends that fire the collective imagination and encourage people to ponder higher values and, in the process, raise humanity to new heights.

THE PROPHET
——— MOHAMMAD'S PART ———

MOHAMMAD WAS A LEADER WHO BROUGHT PEACE AND prosperity to his people. By all accounts, he was a humble and generous man who lived a short life filled with glory and tragedy. By his early twenties, this orphaned boy was already displaying characteristics that would mark him out in history.

His strong sense of social justice was made apparent in both his dealings as a merchant and, with an interest in diverse intellectual, emotional, and spiritual matters, his innate ability to bring about reconciliation in the most difficult situations.

While taking a caravan across the desert, the founder of the Islamic tradition met his adored first wife, Khadijah, who was a number of years his senior and a successful merchant in her own right. She proposed marriage and he accepted, thereby entering into one of the most important relationships of his life. She was not only his wife, but also his mentor, schooling him in the ways of the Merchant Priesthood.

After the death of Khadijah, Mohammad married his second wife, Âishah. When his companions asked him whom he most loved in the whole world, Mohammad always answered, Âishah. Hearing him announce his love for a woman was deeply surprising for his companions, being a new concept for them, having always thought of love in terms of the manly camaraderie between warriors. So, they asked him which man he loved most, to which he answered Abû Bakr, Âishah's father, a gentleman well known for his sensitivity. Having been brought up on patriarchal values and expecting Mohammed to choose a warrior or a champion, this answer confounded his companions. They were simply not accustomed to the admiration of what they considered to be feminine qualities within a man.

His enemies taunted him about the fact that he had only daughters and no sons, while they had been given sons to perpetuate their patriarchal ways. Allah consoled the Prophet with a message: "We have given thee al-Kawthar." *Al-Kawthar* is a sacred pool of life-giving water found in Paradise, a profoundly feminine symbol, representing a heavenly exaltation of the feminine principles over the patriarchal principles of society. *Al-Kawthar* is derived from the same Arabic root as *kathîr*, meaning "Abundance," a quality of the Divine Feminine.

A major part of Mohammad's teaching was about returning the sacred and the feminine to a culture where chauvinism and the warrior mentality had overtaken society. After his own awakening, Mohammad would go on to preach: "None honors women except he who is honorable — and none despises them except he who is despicable... The best of you is the one who is best toward women... Woman is the world's finest treasure."

Sadly, Islam is often portrayed as a masculine, patriarchal faith. Actually, the opposite is true if one truly researches the essence of the teachings. If you really examine Mohammad's words, you will discover the integral, core importance of the feminine in the original teachings of Islam.

Recently, there has been a lot of controversy over how to reshape Christianity to include the feminine on the Divine level, but from my research it seems that in Islam it has never been an issue, since it was present from the beginning, especially in Sufism.

Mohammad settled in Mecca, a town made sacred by the Ka'bah, a black rock that is housed in a covered structure. It is said this rock fell from the sky during the time of Abraham. According to some historical accounts, the Ka'aba was previously regarded as a female deity. Along the building's side stood the many different deities of the warring tribes of Arabia. Because it was the major center of trade and communication for Arabia, Mecca was one of the few places where a longstanding truce had been enacted. Within the city, tribes could worship their individual totems and observe their rites and rituals in peace.

Mohammad enjoyed meeting the varied pilgrims and merchants for whom the Ka'bah was a destination and his reputation as an arbitrator of disputes grew. He also enjoyed an ongoing dialogue between the many Christian and Jewish scholars and mystics he befriended.

Mohammad also spent much time alone, wandering the hills above the bustling town and meditating in the Cave of Hira. It was here that Mohammad experienced Allah/God and the teachings and Beauty that became the Holy Quran.

In Arabic, God or Allah has no form and is neither masculine nor feminine, but rather conceived as the perfect, omnipotent, omniscient, originating, and underlying force of the universe. It was Mohammad's experience of this that would start a revolution of tolerance, unity, forgiveness, trust, and Beauty, which would spread via faith and Commerce to three continents and eventually the world.

Let us consider Muslim or *Sharia* law with regard to economics and Commerce. Unlike our current system, Islamic law expressly forbids paying interest on deposits of cash. According to Islamic economic jurisprudence, *riba* or "interest" is illegal, considered to be a major sin. Going into debt is likewise illegal.

It is believed people should invest in their own businesses or in the business endeavors of family and friends, in order to keep the money in circulation, improve the community, help families, create opportunities, reduce or prevent unemployment, and build vital connections between people and cultures. Rather than turning money over to the bank or sinking it into bonds, people are encouraged to invest in family and friends who have innovative ideas. This is in accord with the teachings of the Prophet, which advise that "two-thirds of your Abundance should come from trade."

Here is a quote from Wikipedia about Islamic banking: "It is banking or banking activity that is consistent with the principles of sharia and its practical application through the development of Islamic economics. Sharia prohibits the fixed or floating payment or acceptance of specific interest or fees (known as *riba*, or usury) for loans of money. Investing in businesses that provide goods or services considered contrary to Islamic principles (mostly meaning businesses related to the sales or production of alcohol, drugs, sex, unfair treatment of animals or nature) is also *haraam* ("sinful and prohibited"). Although these principles have been applied in varying degrees by historical Islamic economies due to lack of Islamic practice, only in the late twentieth century were a number of Islamic banks formed to apply these principles to private or semiprivate commercial institutions within the Muslim community."

Islamic banking has the same purpose as conventional banking: to make money for the banking institute by lending out capital. But that is not the sole purpose either. Adherence to Islamic law and ensuring fair play is also at the core of Islamic banking. Because Islam forbids simply lending out money at interest, Islamic rules on transactions (known as *Fiqh al-Muamalat*) have been created to prevent it. The basic principle of Islamic banking is based on risk-sharing, which is a component of trade rather than risk-transfer, which is seen in conventional banking. Islamic banking introduces concepts such as profit sharing (*Mudharabah*), safekeeping (*Wadiah*), joint venture (*Musharakah*), cost plus (*Murabahah*), and leasing (*Ijar*).

Mohammad, a man of his time, was awake to and aware of the needs and feelings of the people and the religious currents of his era. Divisions were deep and damaging in the tribal culture of Arabia and Mohammad's experience of the oneness of all beings enabled a new way of thinking and responding to life's challenges. His emphasis lay always in the unity of all, thereby creating acceptance, trust, connectedness, and Beauty as a basis of existence. A merchant's life and livelihood were dramatically improved by the embodiment of these qualities, which, when coupled with Commerce, spawned a vibrant, diverse, and groundbreaking Islamic culture. Mohammad held a vision similar to that of the pharaoh Akhenaten: the dream of a spiritual society connected through Commerce and united by one God.

For the most part, the spread of Islam was welcomed by people as a liberation from oppressive rulers and an overblown priesthood. Muslims were careful not to break down local cultures or lore. They practiced only tolerance, with Islam allowing a direct connection to divinity, sparing the people's precious resources from a gorged and greedy clergy.

Wherever Muslims went, they maintained, improved, or established infrastructure, building mosques, schools, and hospitals and creating great Beauty. As stated in the Koran: *"Above all things, Allah is beauty and thus beauty is transcendent."*

The Purpose of the Islamic State, as suggested by the Prophet Mohammad, is the establishment, maintenance, and development of those virtues by which the Creator of the Universe wishes human life to be enriched. In Islam, the State is not intended for political administration, nor for the fulfillment of the collective will of any particular set of people. The aim is to encourage the qualities of purity, Beauty, Goodness, virtue, success, and Prosperity, which God wanted to flourish in the life of the people, while avoiding exploitation and injustice.

On his deathbed, Mohammad recommended to his followers to choose the best amongst them to lead after him. He made it clear that merit rather than bloodline was the key to leadership, advocating the concept of meritocracy, as opposed to a full democracy. He believed that a fully developed democracy of the people required humanity to attain a higher level of education and emotional maturity than existed at that time.

True democracy, as promoted by the Merchant Priests, is an evolutionary process, which grows and evolves, becoming "true" with the attainment of emotional maturity. The Priests knew that the concept of creating universal equality is an ideal to strive toward, developing in stages. It couldn't be forced onto a people who had not yet reached a certain level of Emotional Intelligence. This is something the Prophet Mohammed was aware of before he died and he therefore didn't try to impose democracy onto his people, advocating instead that the person to replace him would be chosen on merit.

In today's world, some Muslims reject democracy, because the Prophet Mohammed did not choose it as a viable path for government. They insist on the concept of meritocracy which, sadly, some confuse with the leadership of the clergy, not realizing that meritocracy is one of the key steps toward democracy.

At the same time, many people around the world are questioning and reconsidering the concept of democracy, acknowledging where the principles are working and where progress still needs to be made.

The Merchant Priesthood understood that the concept of democracy is an ideal that is in a constant state of evolution, changing with the times, reflecting the emotional and spiritual maturity of the people. The relatively recent Western democratic experiment is itself still evolving. Although in many ways it has been successful, it has also failed in some respects, particularly where corruption and bipartisanism continue to cripple governments.

For us, the following quote by Terry Tempest Williams represents some of the higher ideals of democracy envisioned by the Merchant Priesthood:

"The human heart is the first home of democracy. It is where we embrace our questions: Can we be equitable? Can we be generous? Can we listen with our whole beings, not just our minds, and offer our attention rather than our opinion? And do we have enough resolve in our hearts to act courageously, relentlessly, without giving up ever — trusting our fellow citizens to join us in our determined pursuit of a living democracy?"

THE KNIGHTS TEMPLAR

ONE OF THE MOST SIGNIFICANT HISTORICAL BRIDGES THE Merchant Priests used to pass the knowledge of Sacred Commerce through the ages from Egypt to now is the Knights Templar. With the decline of Egypt, the mantle was handed to the Hebrews, then to the Essenes and down through the ages, until the energy current carried by the Priesthood was eventually transferred to a special order of knights: the Knights Templar. Born in the Middle Ages, this sect is perhaps the best example of a holy order of monastic warriors, whose discipline was the unification of sacred and secular activities within the context of banking and trading. Again, as with the Egyptians, these men knew that Commerce was a path to the sacred heart, when practiced in a sacred context.

The Knights Templar did more than we, or they, will ever know to usher us into the modern world we recognize today. As peace-brokers for kings and popes alike, they were the real-life counterparts to King Arthur's knights and the embodiment of the Holy Grail. Amongst their ranks, noble blood always gave deference to merit, thus usurping the old paradigm whereby power was automatically passed down via inheritance. In spirituality, as opposed to religion, the only hierarchy that exists is the hierarchy of love and support. Bloodlines and "the Divine right of kings" no longer reign supreme. Mutual consideration and courtesy are high values to this emergent class of men who, in turn, become concerned with being "gentle-men" embodying Goodness and protecting the people.

Having assumed the mission of protecting the pilgrim routes to Jerusalem, the Knights Templar's reputation was — and is — unique in the annals of history. They exemplified balance of character within a single individual, where the perfect harmony suggested by the yin-yang symbol is given expression in the gentleness of a lamb and the ferocity of a lion.

The Knights Templar's origins can be traced to co-founder and first Grand Master, Hugues de Payens, who traveled east to the Holy Land during the Christian crusades in the early part of the twelfth century, as vassal to Count Hugh of Champagne. The richest of all the feudal lords at that time, Count Hugh was reportedly four to five times wealthier than the King of France himself and strongly influenced by religious mysticism and reformist Benedictine thought.

When Count Hugh returned to France, nine of his vassals — one of them being Hugues de Payens — were told to remain in Jerusalem at the Temple Mount. Convinced that he himself carried the bloodline of Jesus, the count charged his vassals with the task of unearthing the Ark of the Covenant and discovering its hidden secrets.

Ever a subject of intrigue and mystery, it is believed that the Ark was carried out of Egypt by Moses and eventually made its way to Jerusalem. Contradictory accounts exist about what happened to the treasured Ark next, although some say it was buried or lost when the Temple of Solomon fell in 586 BC. It's also suggested that it was safely spirited away when Jerusalem fell in 1291 AD. The earliest written copies of Masonic ritual claim that the Ark was found in a cave on the Temple of the Mount.

The Temple of the Mount in Jerusalem was the spiritual center of the Middle East. The Wailing Wall finds the Hebrew people worshipping on one side and the Muslims streaming into the mosque on the other.

Count Hugh's vassals — who subsequently became the Knights Templar — spent ten years fulfilling their assignment to dig beneath the Temple Mount in search of the Ark and its secrets. Even Count Hugh himself returned to Jerusalem in order to join the special order of the Knights Templar and their search for the Ark, giving up both his title and his wife. Templar records speak of "hidden treasure," not in the shape of jewels or gold coins, but in the form of secret knowledge.

What we find most fascinating is that these men who went in search of the Ark of the Covenant founded an order that rose to great power and prominence in the years that followed. Could it be that these men actually found the secret scrolls hidden by the Essenes and acquired specialist knowledge of the Merchant Priesthood that can be traced to the spiritual current we are now calling Sacred Commerce?

We believe that these scrolls contain the secrets of Emotional Alchemy, along with some of the highest spiritual truths for personal transformation and transcendence. Firstly, the truth that we create our own reality, rather than having a preordained destiny handed down to us by God, which we have to accept without question. Secondly, that we can have a direct relationship with God, without priests or religion. And thirdly, our relationship with God can go beyond one of fear or even love, through to a relationship of Partnership.

Any of these truths would have been blasphemous — and this holds true even today. This is why the Knights kept their discoveries hidden from the church and the crown and practiced the spiritual truths in secret.

Perhaps what they discovered was not a bloodline, but instructions on how to align their activities with the implicit Divine order? Would this explain how they amassed such great wealth and power in the years that followed? And what if even then their activities favored freeing the masses from the oppression of poverty and war, rather than supporting the sole authority of church or crown?

Might this explain why they were such a clear threat to the existing power structure and why both the French crown and the pope rallied to strip them of the power, possibly passed down to them through Moses from Akhenaten?

Many claim that these "great secrets," if revealed, may undermine our fundamental view of Christianity. Some see this to mean the revelation of the story of the bloodline of Jesus and the mysteries of Mary Magdalene and the sacred feminine in Christianity.

We'd like to dispel some of the suspicion around the Freemasons and other so-called "secret societies" or societies with secrets. Although power-hungry secret societies did and still do exist, this does not mean they are all the same. Many were and are uniquely benevolent. Seen through the lens of evolution, it would appear that certain individuals have been given specialized training and knowledge, making them more adept at carrying the torch of awareness forward, and living to serve all equally.

During dark times, fearful for their lives, these individuals, renaissance men and woman, went underground — or, in modern terms, "disappeared below the radar." When prevailing beliefs, as promoted by the ruling class or the church, sought to extinguish the light of awareness, be that basic literacy, the tools of Commerce, or a democratic mindset, these men and women had to conceal what they knew or work behind the scenes, due to the very real threat of persecution.

The Knights Templar do not have a completely untarnished record in history. The undoubtedly sincere ideals of the wise and the good Knights were unfortunately not always upheld by every member of the order.

At this time in European history, for some of the men involved, being a knight had regrettably lost some of its original meaning and value. For them, the qualities of chivalry had faded under the strain of so much fighting and battle.

While in Jerusalem as Count Hugh's vassal, Hugues de Payens encountered the Muslim concept of chivalry, the Bedouin principles of *al-furusiyyah* (horsemanship) and *muru'ah* (manliness and honor, emphasizing brotherhood, courage, generosity, and loyalty). This encounter also regenerated and reinvigorated the sense of chivalry in the hearts of those men, who had temporarily lost touch with their deeper values of Goodness.

In the deserts of Arabia, a man in Arab dress — sword in scabbard and spear in hand, riding his pure Arabian horse across the sands — has long been a symbol of justice and protection. The Arabs are said to have been amongst the first to practice a chivalrous code of honor as a way of life. From long before the birth of Christ and prior to the advent of Islam, chivalry was a recognized social institution on the Arabian Peninsula.

Unlike the Greeks, Romans, and Persians, Arabs fought their wars fairly and, for the most part, without treachery. Champions fought in front of both armies and battles often took place by appointment. Arabian chivalry was a code of ethics, life, and social structure that grew until it became synonymous with the quest for freedom and justice, as well as a man fighting to the death to protect the women and children.

Since time immemorial, the chivalrous Arabian knight protected his womenfolk, providing the prototype for the medieval European "knight in shining armor." Protecting the good repute and honor of women, family, and tribe was a basic requirement for an Arabian knight. In the time prior to and following the birth of Islam, women were very important in society. They inspired the poet to sing and the warrior to fight.

These men became knights via their reputation, rather than being formally "knighted," as later was the custom in Europe. Their courage, dignity, and noble deeds made them treasures to their people, with their adventures and feats becoming the subject of many tales and legends.

Over the next two hundred years, the "Order of the Poor Knights of Christ and the Temple of Solomon" — later shortened to the "Knights Templar" — became the most powerful and secretive organization in history, amassing great wealth and owing allegiance to none but the pope.

Many features of the international monetary exchange system originated with the Templars. Chapters functioned as schools of diplomacy, with advanced degrees in Commerce and finance. The vast estates owned by the Order of the Knights Templar were sanctuaries for all who needed protection. Individual knights took vows of poverty and refused to accumulate personal wealth. Instead, they used their funds to leverage land deals and make advances in agriculture, supporting new construction, building expansion and the modest beginnings of industry. In this way, the kings of Europe became indebted to the order.

Charged with ensuring safe passage to those making a pilgrimage to the Holy Land from Europe, the Knights devised a system utilizing a coded chit, representing the amount of money the pilgrim was carrying — a clear precursor to the modern-day credit card or check.

In short, the Knights put their wealth to work in service of the whole. Exempt from excommunication and all papal decrees not specifically addressed to them, the Templars also managed to free themselves from any tax liability. As "defenders of church and cross," they became a separate social, political, and religious order that transcended all legal and economic lines. Although their military presence in the East diminished once the Muslims reclaimed Jerusalem, the Templar's influence continued to be strong. In charge of thousands of houses around Europe, they were business managers, farm and vineyard owners, and held safety deposit boxes, in which people stored their valuables and wealth.

Their unique status as a sovereign state with a standing army that knew no borders was a source of great tension to some, especially King Philip the Fair of France, who had amassed a sizeable debt to the order while warring with England.

In an attempt to resolve this tension and erase his debt to the Knights, the king devised a plan to merge all the religious orders — including the Templars — and form "the Knights of Jerusalem," with a French prince at the helm. When his "merger and acquisitions" plan failed, the king launched a massive campaign against the Templars, accusing them of magic and heresy.

On October 13, 1307, the king ordered every Templar in France to be arrested; some stories suggest the arrests took place at a grand party hosted by the king himself. Over the course of the next few years, hundreds of Knights were tortured and put to death or imprisoned.

The last Grand Master, Jacques de Molay, was burnt at the stake in 1314 and it is generally assumed that the order ended with his death. However, some of the Knights Templar are believed to have escaped persecution; they, their treasure, their enormous fleet of ships, and their mysterious secrets are said to have mysteriously disappeared.

This sudden demise of the Templars in Europe, whose goodwill and protection the common people had come to depend upon, sent a ripple of many revolutions across the continent that ultimately led to the French Revolution, the weakening of the Catholic Church, and the spread of democratic ideals.

Legend suggests that some of the Knights sailed a fleet of some twenty ships to Scotland, finding safe harbor there. The Scottish king, Robert the Bruce, had been excommunicated by Rome and did not answer to the pope or fall under his jurisdiction. Soon after the arrival of the Knights, Masonic guilds began appearing all over Scotland.

It is believed that another group managed to travel east to Switzerland, taking their secret knowledge and treasure with them. As luck or the Divine Plan would have it, their escape coincided with Switzerland's formation as a conglomeration of provinces. The early Swiss records speak of the mysterious appearance of "white knights," who helped the local population gain their independence from foreign domination. The Templar cross is still incorporated today in many of the flags of the Swiss cantons, as are two other prominent Templar symbols: the keys and the lamb. In settling in Switzerland, the Knights Templar had a significant impact on it becoming the banking and global finance center that it continues to be even today.

In early times, as with the Internet today, navigation was crucial. The Knights Templar inherited an unbroken line of technical knowledge. The Merchant Priesthood — manifest here as an order of knights — always carried the keys to this knowledge, in the form of the latest technological know-how.

While in the modern day, we swap domains, servers, and Internet access points, the Knights owned large fleets and elaborate maps. Long before the development of the chronometer, they were able to circumnavigate the world, due to their ability to fix longitudinal positions. Using their knowledge and principles, some of their ships reached as far away as Nova Scotia centuries before Columbus reached the Americas. Some historians believe that Isaac Newton, Vasco De Gama, and Columbus himself had connections to the order and some evidence even suggests that the Knights discovered America some eighty years before Columbus.

Regarding modern-day navigation, consider the remarkable success of the American multinational corporation,

Google. Its mission statement from the outset was "to organize the world's information and make it universally accessible and useful." This visionary company is clearly aligned with the aims of the Merchant Priesthood.

More than any single search engine on the Internet, *Google* has leveled the playing field by giving everyone the ability to navigate the World Wide Web and access more information than ever before in history. At the same time, it has allowed people to monetize their information, experience, and creations, providing a new avenue along which Abundance can flow. As we work toward completion of this manuscript, *Google* is in the process of scanning every page of every book in every library, thus making the knowledge in those libraries accessible to the furthest corners of the world at the touch of a button.

It seems highly likely that the Knights had early contact with the Native American Iroquois nation in Canada. Legend tells of them contributing to the Iroquois' "Great Law of Peace," a democratic system of checks and balances between the tribes that helped them to maintain general peace.

According to Adrian White Bear of the *Idle No More Community,* the "Great Law of Peace" Confederacy arose centuries ago amongst separate, warring communities, as a way to create and share harmony, unity, and respect. Implicit in Iroquois political philosophy is a commitment to the highest principles of human liberty. The Great Law's recognition of individual liberty and justice surpasses any European parallel.

Faith-keeper Oren Lyons, in Onondaga, states that the Great Law of Peace includes "freedom of speech, freedom of religion, [and] the right of women to participate in government. Separation of power in government and checks and balances within government are traceable to our Iroquois constitution — ideas learned by the colonists."

The central idea underlying Iroquois political philosophy is that peace is the will of the Creator and the ultimate spiritual goal and natural order among humans. The principles of their government embodied in the Great Law of Peace were transmitted by a historical figure called the Peacemaker. His teachings emphasize the power of Reason to assure Righteousness, Justice, and Health among humans. Peace came to the Iroquois, not through war and conquest, but through the exercise of Reason guided by the spiritual mind. The Iroquois League is based not on force of arms or rule of law, but spiritual concepts of natural law applied to human society.

Benjamin Franklin learned of this indigenous constitution and allowed it to influence his thinking as he participated in the debate that led to the writing of the American Constitution. So, the Templars influenced the Iroquois, who in turn carried the seed — adding their own wisdom and experience — before handing it on to the next great experiment in democracy: the United States of America.

The Iroquois were not the only indigenous Americans to play a part in world affairs. The Incas also played a key role in the establishment of capitalism, when they flooded Spain and the rest of Europe with silver.

When Spanish conquistadors went to Peru in search of gold, the Merchant Priests of the Incas resolved to reveal to them the location of the Silver Mountains. For centuries, legends described how the Peruvian shamans told their people to leave untouched the vast stores of this rare mineral they had found in the earth; they foresaw a time when the silver would be needed for a higher purpose — and that time duly came.

The search for gold was the motivation for the conquistadors to travel from Spain to South America, supported by the unholy alliance between royalty and the church. The Peruvian Merchant Priests were aware of the ravaging effects of the conquistadors' expedition on South American communities and how it would continue to spread unless urgent action was taken.

Up until then, gold had been the main currency and was exclusively in the hands of royalty and the church; everybody else bartered with sheep, crops, crafts, services, or whatever they had. The Merchant Priests' intention was to curtail the excesses of these two powerful institutions, which were the source of so much misery especially in South America and Europe.

The Merchant Priests led the Spanish to a virtual mountain of silver and, shortly thereafter, the mineral began pouring into Europe. This development was absolutely necessary for "leveling society's playing field." In time, silver became a form of universal currency for the emerging "middle class," effectively shifting the economic base to the people; no longer was the aristocracy the exclusive holder of the purse strings. The newfound prosperity and sense of freedom enjoyed by the people enabled them to educate themselves, capitalize new ideas and develop new products, which in turn allowed them to gain more power and, ultimately, to stand up against the excesses of both church and royalty.

This sense of empowerment reverberated throughout Europe, later influencing revolutionary thoughts, philosophies, and consciousness, where people began to demand a more economically balanced and democratic society.

The introduction of silver also mitigated the appetite for gold in Europe, at a time when gold fever was heating up the economy. A beautiful illustration of our interdependence with the mineral kingdoms, silver in effect "cooled down" the collective psychic state of Europeans. By introducing silver — a feminine, cooling energy — in industrial quantities, the Merchant Priests balanced the overheated gold-standard economy.

Important to note in this context is that the introduction of silver — the poor man's currency — eventually supported the expansion of trade allowing for a middle class to emerge, which eventually bankrolled and protected democracy.

Although the presence of the Merchant Priests among the Incas cannot be tracked historically, this move — by men of their priestly class — certainly evidences a rarified sensibility and understanding of collective human behavior and economics.

TULIP MANIA: THE FIRST
GREAT MARKET BUBBLE

ONE OF THE GREAT STORIES IN THE HISTORY OF COMMERCE is the tulip mania that seized the Netherlands, circa 1630. What few people understand is that the Merchant Priesthood was working behind the scenes. This time, they worked with the plant kingdom — and among their allies were potatoes and tulips.

The water mains in Northern Europe were liberated, when farmers began to plant potatoes instead of wheat, a water-intensive crop. The water that had previously been monopolized by agriculture then became available for an entirely new phenomenon: generating electricity. As the Industrial Revolution began its gestation period, France, Holland, and Germany, each in its own way, started sending out ships to colonize what they considered to be "the territories."

Fighting between France and England started to block — and, in some cases, even destroy — the trade routes. Previously, trade had flowed freely, but with imperialism on the rise and European powers intent on monopolizing the world, trade routes were cut and shortened, inhibiting Commerce. Excessive demand in Europe made supplies elsewhere scarce.

The Merchant Priesthood in the Ottoman Empire became involved when they responded to a request from their South African brothers, who were suffering at the hands of the Dutch. Together, they devised an unusually clever intervention — a plan that would nudge down Holland's GNP (gross national product), a measure of the wealth of a nation. Their aim was to reduce the available capital the Dutch had to finance their imperialistic ambitions, by introducing something entirely new into the European economy. This move was not so much an economic ploy to hijack their excess wealth, as it was a means of redistribution. The Merchant Priests also sought to tame and balance the self-importance of the European powers, because their emotional inflation was threatening to monopolize global trade.

When a leading botanist from Leiden went on a trade visit to Constantinople, he had no idea of the mellifluous adventure on which he was about to embark. The tulip mania he was about to trigger is often cited in histories as an example of collective mania and obsession. The effects of the tulip flower were actually well known in ancient Greece, where they were used in the Eleusinian Mysteries to bring on temporary amnesia.

The Merchant Priesthood knew that if the tulip flower made its way to Europe, one of two things would happen. Either the delicate perfume of the flower would serve to calm the collective economic and emotional frenzy of the times or the population would become obsessed with the flower. In the case of the latter, they foresaw people becoming so obsessed with acquisition of the tulip that it would cause a speculative bubble, which would eventually, inevitably crash. Either way, they knew that a certain amount of financial heat would be taken out of the system.

The notion of a flower scent being so powerful as to affect an entire culture might seem rather far-fetched. Certainly, a huge quantity of the blooming anomaly would be required to have an effect. However, consider the current fascination with flower essences, essential oils, and aroma-therapy, or even the vast marketing budgets the perfume industry puts behind their newest *Passion* or *Taboo*. In this light, the thought of a flower having hypnotic olfactory power over people becomes less absurd.

The tulip bulb was brought north to Europe just after the turn of the sixteenth century. Within a few short decades, the flower was in high demand all across the continent and, by the 1630s, demand had reached a fever pitch. In the Netherlands, people were selling everything they had just to purchase a few bulbs. At the peak of the bubble, one humble tulip bulb was selling for the equivalent of twenty tons of cheese. A seventeenth-century father might have trouble finding a suitor for his daughter if the tulip was not promi-nent in her dowry. For a few years, the bulbs themselves became an alternative form of currency. For example, they were often traded like stocks at the mansion of an aristocrat in Amsterdam, whose name was La Bourse. To this day, the Paris stock exchange bears his name.

In one of the most popular novels of the 1800s, Alexandre Dumas tells the tale of *The Black Tulip*. Set in the city of Haarlem in the Netherlands, the novel tells of fierce competition between the country's best gardeners for a prize of 100,000 florins, promised to the person who could grow a black tulip.

Truly black flowers are unknown in nature and yet twentieth-century black tulips, bred by horticulturalists — such as the African Queen, Black Diamond, Black Hero, and Arabian Mystery, which are actually deep shades of ruby-red, mahogany, burgundy wine, and violet purple — evoke a sense of lusty drama to this very day.

This flurry of economic activity had a number of downstream effects that demonstrate the unusual role of the Merchant Priesthood in cultural evolution. As we have said before, this unique ministry had set its sights less on "saving souls" and more on providing tools for Commerce that allow society to rise out of poverty to enjoy Abundance and Prosperity, so that it can pursue the highest virtues of Beauty, Goodness, and Truth. How did tulip mania serve these ends? In effect, it led to the first futures market, which eventually gave birth to the stock market.

The stock market allows people with small amounts of capital to invest and get onto a larger playing field, a privilege formerly reserved for big capital. This innovation allows the individual to gain from the success of large companies, creating a participatory economy that lets many levels of society prosper. As an example, let's look at what happens when a large company sells shares or stock. They raise money by selling to hundreds of thousands of small shareholders, allowing the average working man to participate in the success and Abundance generated by big capital. The small investor is the progeny of the stock market. One share gives him a voice; he can now participate in a larger commercial activity than were he to work solely on his own.

The stock market is also a tool that allows entrepreneurs with new ideas and innovations to raise needed capital. This in turn also redistributes wealth, because the rich are not the only ones who can get richer; the middle class can grow their bank accounts, portfolios, and assets as well.

Just how did the lovely tulip flower set off this domino effect? As the flowers were imported from Crete, it took quite a long time for them to get to Northern Europe. Shipments were purchased in advance, creating what is called today the "futures market." It was not at all uncommon for 60-90% of the tulips to die in transit, which meant the price could go up or down by as much as ten times. In effect, the futures market has always been an economic betting game — or in this case "tulip roulette." Among both the aristocracy and the emerging middle class, people were so keen to obtain the coveted flower, many sold off their assets at below market price in order to speculate on the tulip market. The poorer sections of society benefited from this dumping of assets.

In 1637, the tulip speculation bubble burst. The heat of the European economy began to cool, all because of the ingenuity and the enchantment wafting up from a brightly colored bloom.

Although this is the story passed on through legend and storytellers, did the Merchant Priesthood really think all this out and strategically plan such an intervention? Was the process conscious or more of an unconscious movement toward an idea that held some vague promise of merit? Perhaps we will never know if silver currency and tulip mania were preconceived as a "big plan" or if they just acted on what they knew and felt in the moment.

What we mean to highlight is simple: the spiritual current toward higher forms of both individual and collective expression has moved humanity throughout time. We affectionately call this current "the Pulse," experiencing its flow and elegant movement in a personal way that might be called "destiny."

THE FOUNDING OF
AMERICA

THE PRINCIPLES OF THE MERCHANT PRIESTHOOD ALSO
played a pivotal role in the founding of America; it was to be
their greatest experiment and achievement. With the birth
of the United States, the new form of governance known
as democracy gained considerable velocity. Thirteen of the
thirty-nine signatories of the Constitution were Freemasons
and nine were amongst the group who drew up the
Declaration of Independence.

This document carries a message much like that of the
French Revolution with its slogan of "Liberty, Fraternity,
and Equality." American revolutionaries added the spiritual
dimension to their dream by including "the pursuit of happiness." As Maslow points out with the Hierarchy of Needs
pyramid, each time you satisfy a need you become happier.
Happiness arises with the successive fulfillment of our needs
from survival to Beauty and is the essence of enlightenment
— or, in Maslow's terms, *the realized self.*

Common to both the French and the American revolutions was the goal of establishing a republican form of
governance that would feature a congress and president
elected by the people. These ideals bear witness to the influence of the Freemasons, who saw themselves as architects of

a new Temple of Solomon, which was destroyed in AD 70 by the Roman emperor Titus.

Among the Freemasons, the Temple symbolized the "New Jerusalem" — the finest and most rarified expression of human nature possible. With the opening of America, the Freemasons resurfaced. It is no coincidence that Washington, D.C. has always been known as "the shining city on the hill." Neither is it a coincidence that the dollar bill shows a truncated pyramid with the cap not yet quite in place. The All Seeing Eye of Wisdom that beams out from the cap will finally be in place when the United States of America is governed and led by the spiritual ideals that were encoded into its founding documents.

Much of this symbolic communication was the work of the Freemasons, who had great hopes for the United States. Considering their history and the persecution of the Knights Templar by King Philip of France, it is easy to understand their allegiance to a republican form of government that adheres to the principles of democracy. Those who crafted the documents that formed this nation truly believed that America had the potential to become the country where church and state could finally be clearly separated.

Given the deeply spiritual intent of the Founding Fathers, the notion of separating church and state always struck me as something of an oxymoron. What I now realize is that their focus was on "church and state," not "spirituality and state." How can governance unfold benevolently without divine guidance and influence? What seems true is that the aim was not so much to separate the secular and the sacred, as it was to create a roadblock for the government from exercising control over people's spirituality.

The treachery seen in France and other parts of Europe, when royalty was in cahoots with the Church, highlighted the folly of mixing these two bedfellows. We still see examples of this around the world.

If spiritual development is the main goal in a person's life, he or she naturally wants to make that dimension of existence available to others. The Founding Fathers aimed at keeping the sphere of spirituality unencumbered. They had a deep sense of spirituality and believed strongly that all individuals should have the right to their own unique relationship with God, controlled neither by the State nor the Church. The Founding Fathers championed spiritual sovereignty by declaring freedom of choice with respect to whatever godhead one might conceive or implore.

Benjamin Franklin was a celebrated member of the Freemasons and a Grand Master at the age of twenty-eight. One of the most well-known Founding Fathers of America, he was also an inventor, diplomat, civic activist, and political and social engineer. In 1727, at the age of twenty-one, he founded the first volunteer association in America, the *Junto*. This lively discussion group was convened to bring together aspiring artisans and tradesmen who shared a commitment to improving themselves, while they simultaneously improved their community.

As the first "convention" of this kind, the *Junto* can be seen as the precursor to the entire self-help and personal growth movement. Their focus on what we would call in today's world "inner and outer ecology" is what made the *Junto* both unique and effective. Philadelphia's volunteer fire department and many other civic-minded service organizations grew out of this group. Franklin also founded the first public library in America, a vision that spread across the land resulting in thousands of libraries gracing even the smallest community. Again, we see the expression of the Merchant Priesthood's mission to level the playing field and bring resources — in this case knowledge and literacy — to the people.

From his late twenties and throughout his thirties — the "midlife" years by eighteenth-century standards — Franklin's trade was that of a printer. In effect, he was an author and publisher — best known for the famous *Poor Richard's Almanac,* still in print over two centuries later, and *The Pennsylvania Gazette.* His eloquent writings significantly contributed to the ideals of democracy and are among the most important works of political theory and philosophy we have.

Franklin was born into a world where suspicion, witch hunts, and slavery dominated human thinking; a world where a lightning strike was seen as punishment from the hand of God, and where a man was expected to simply accept his station in life. In Franklin's case, that meant a life of poverty as a member of the working class. However, his soul force and unique genius propelled him far beyond the limitations of his birth and the dominant view of reality at the time. A wealthy man by the age of thirty, Franklin made innumerable contributions to eighteenth-century society, not the least of which was protection from the hand of God, when it came down from the sky with supreme vengeance.

In those days, if a lightning bolt struck a house or farm, it was seen as punishment; a clear indication that the owner had committed some sin. The community would protect the neighboring homes from fire and simply let the house

struck by lightning burn to the ground. Franklin invented
what we now know as the lightning rod, which not only
provided protection, but shook the very foundation of the
prevailing chauvinistic worldview that presupposed an absolute and punishing authority lording over us from on high.
If free will allows us to protect ourselves from the hand of
God, what else might we do with this marvelous capacity? How else can we work in Partnership with the powers
that be?

What is important to note about Franklin's life, in the
context of Sacred Commerce, is his generosity and "gift-
economy" attitude. Although he was a copious inventor,
Franklin never patented so much as one of his inventions —
not out of martyrdom or lack of interest in his own financial
well-being, but out of his zeal to speed the evolution of
his countrymen and his desire to have impact. He was a
special breed of entrepreneur as can be seen in the following statement from his autobiography: "[As] we enjoy great
advantages from the invention of others, we should be glad
of an opportunity to serve others by any invention of ours;
and this we should do freely and generously."

By creating a bastion for democracy on the continent
of North America, the Freemasons took a stand for economic, intellectual, and spiritual freedom, fulfilling one of
the dreams of the Merchant Priesthood.

TODAY'S KNIGHTS OF COMMERCE: THE RISE OF THE _____ GLOBAL CITIZEN _____

TODAY'S MERCHANT PRIESTS MAY NOT KNOW THEMSELVES by that name or as the "Knights of Commerce," but they are men and women changing the face of society and humanity by leveling the playing field in new and innovative ways. We will look at just a couple of them as examples, even though we know there are many more. Maybe you are one of them?

As we have mentioned, Nobel Prize winner Dr. Mohammad Yunus is one of the first economists and bankers to sit in the company of Nelson Mandela, the Dalai Lama, Desmond Tutu, Mother Teresa, and others, whose work has advanced the cause of peace.

As a university professor, Dr. Yunus wondered why economic theory had so little to do with the reality of slow economic growth in poor nations like his own country, Bangladesh.

In 1974, he met a young craftswoman who made lovely bamboo stools. Due to the fact that she was not an "independent contractor," to use our terms, but instead had to rely on someone else to provision her with bamboo, the woman could only earn two cents per day. With a simple six-dollar loan, Dr. Yunus helped her to rise up to the middle class, by increasing her daily income to $1.25. In effect, by enabling her to buy wholesale bamboo herself, the six dollars allowed her to go into business for herself.

In 1979, Dr Yunus founded the first microlending bank — a bank whose focus was loaning small amounts of money to people in poor rural areas, primarily women. The Grameen Bank not only lends money to the poor, it is also majority-owned by the borrowers themselves. Their success has been phenomenal. By 1996, they had loaned more in rural areas than all the other banks combined.

According to their site at *Grameen-info.org*, as of 2011 the Grameen Bank has 2,565 branches. It works in 81,379 villages. Total staff is 22,124. Total amount of loan disbursed by Grameen Bank, since inception, is $11.35 billion. Out of this, $10.11 billion has been repaid. Current amount of outstanding loans stands at $968.31 million. Total number of borrowers is 8.35 million, and 96% of them are women. Loan recovery rate is 96.67%. All its funds come from the deposits it collects from the borrowers and non-borrowers — and it routinely makes a profit. It now has affiliate organizations around the world, including America, which shows a lot of current activity at their site (*Grameenamerica.org*) as of this writing.

In an attempt to explode the myth that microcredit does not work for the "bottom poor," Grameen Bank launched a program to give loans exclusively to beggars, particularly generational beggars. The bank invites them to carry a collection of popular consumer items, financed by Grameen Bank, when they go out to beg. They can both sell and beg; it is their choice. As of 2011, over 111,296 beggars had joined the program —with a typical loan amounting to ten dollars — and 80% of the amount disbursed had already been paid off.

Dr. Yunus believes that we can create a poverty-free world, with the basic ingredient to overcome poverty packed inside each poor person, and that all we need to do is help the person unleash his or her energy and creativity.

Credit is the last hope left to those faced with absolute poverty. That is why Muhammad Yunus believes that the right to credit should be recognized as a fundamental human right. His work goes far deeper than financial health, being profoundly involved in restoring dignity, hope, and personal worth to those people generally forgotten by society. His belief in them has inspired many others to believe in them as well, but most importantly, it has inspired them to believe in themselves — a priceless gift.

The microlending movement has spread from Bangladesh across the globe, opening opportunities for mostly poor women and their families. Dr. Yunus' personal dream is to see poverty and homelessness banished to legend, to be learned about only in museums and libraries.

Another of the most successful business ventures on earth began when a lone bank manager asked some tough questions that sparked a massive mutation in the practice of free enterprise. Every time you pull out your *Visa* card, you participate in a quiet revolution that began in 1968, when one man led a historical move to level the playing field for merchants across the globe. When Dee Hock convinced Bank of America to relinquish ownership and control of their credit card program in favor of a non-stock membership company, equally owned by its member banks, a new species of corporation began to evolve. Inducted into both the Business Hall of Fame and *Money* magazine's Hall of Fame, Dee Hock busted chauvinism's individualistic paradigm at the corporate level.

Decades before the birth of the Internet, Dee Hock was one of the first "Knights of E-Commerce." Like the Merchant Priest of old, Dee Hock did humanity a great service by paving the way for more equality in the marketplace. He developed the concept of a global system for the electronic exchange of value and a unique new form of organization for that purpose: a decentralized, non-stock, for-profit membership institution to be owned by financial institutions throughout the world.

Prior to the *Bank Americard*, predecessor to the *Visa* card — today's ticket-to-ride on the rails of Commerce everywhere — only big vendors could do business in the credit-card game. The local coffee shop or pottery store could only complete a transaction in cash or by accepting the ever-dubious personal check. A small machine that instantly approved and completed a financial transaction did not exist when the flower children of the 1960s came of age. Hock's curiosity and courage changed all this. Today, a single mother who makes quilts and kids' pajamas in her spare time can readily set up a vendor booth at a music festival and sell her wares to anyone who holds a *Visa* card.

Dee Hock asserts that the worldwide success of *Visa International* is due to its chaotic structure. At the time of publishing his book, *The Birth of the Chaordic Age* (1999), *Visa* was owned by 22,000 member banks, which were in competition with each other for 750 million customers and had to cooperate with each other by honoring one another's

$1.25 trillion transactions annually, across borders and currencies. Today, the *Visa* organization that Hock founded is not only performing brilliantly, it is also almost mythic, one of only two examples that experts regularly cite to illustrate how the dynamic principles of chaos theory can be applied to business.

This move was not unlike the creation of coin and currency, which birthed the middle class and fostered a new wave of merchants, expanding the domain of mercantilism. We now see yet another wave of this type with the creation of *eBay*, *PayPal*, and shopping carts that make it easy to conduct commerce via the Internet.

The Internet offers one of the most challenging and exciting opportunities the human race has ever encountered; it is the means by which we may finally be able to bring harmony, spiritual balance, and abundance to bear for all.

By its very nature, the Web demands collaboration, invites participation, and encourages autonomy simultaneously, allowing individual differences to be highlighted and monetized. *Party-cipation* provides the lubricant for collaboration, encouraging Partnerships that coalesce and then dissolve with each new project. The Web opens us to the inevitability of change, propelling the spread and deepening the ideal of democracy. In short order, all across the globe, we may see democratic systems forming across a far wider spectrum of shades and colors than those with which we are currently familiar.

Some countries have tried to restrict the Internet since its inception, but these attempts are failing. Governments are realizing they have to choose between becoming part of the global village and allowing their people to become Global Citizens, or miss the boat of cultural evolution.

Perhaps the most important feature introduced into society by the Internet is the element of transparency. Few are the secrets that hide beyond the reach of *Google* and *YouTube*. Who would have imagined an information age, wherein a weapon of mass deconstruction would bear a name like *Chrome*? Or where watchdogs like *Smoking Gun* (*thesmokinggun.com*) or *Snopes* (*snopes.com*) would keep us abreast of the latest hoax, smokescreen, or scandal. No hope, no prayer, not even the most elaborate cloaking device can hide from the public what is really happening, when even ten-year-olds carry cellular phones with built-in video cameras in their hip pocket.

Far from a police state, what we are witnessing is the emergence of a transparent and intimate state. Open, undisguised, and increasingly *honest* government becomes inevitable and all but unavoidable. A truly Global Citizenry looms large on our horizon.

Even the world's foremost Web analysts cannot predict where the Internet will take us. The medium itself is a blank screen. Like any technology, it is neither good nor evil, but rather reflective of how it is used. More and more, the Internet reveals itself as the screen onto which we project our character, motivations, and dreams. Ultimately, as is true with any human creation, we shall simply behold our own reflection on the Internet. This is why, for the Knights of E-Commerce, it becomes so urgent to use the Web in ways that further all that is most ennobling in humanity — that which facilitates prosperity, peace, and conscious evolution.

The way the Web reaches into everything is another clue to its potential universal, even spiritual, character. It is like nature, in the manner that all things are interconnected. In this way, by relating all parts to a larger whole, the Web has realized an innate inclination towards "systems" and "ecological" principles. The Web can tell us about the origins of a particular product, the research that went into it, or even the degree to which its production and constituents may have harmed life.

With the power of the Web at our fingertips, we can choose to become more aware of the values we are buying into when we purchase a product or service. We have an influence on the life of a product, given that our vote — to buy or not to buy — directly impacts a product's existence. "Knowledge is Freedom," so the saying goes. The Web gives us the freedom of informed choice, putting us in the larger picture and making that larger picture available to anyone who asks the right questions. For this reason, the Web is a call for responsibility and responsible choices. Above all, because of its equally great potential to deluge us with too much information, the Web is a wake-up call to our powers of discernment.

Finally, the Web has also helped to spread the impact and manifestation of the dream of the Merchant Priesthood, well beyond its initial participants — indeed, well beyond those who consciously aspire to be of service.

Throughout history, the Merchant Priests — whether men or women, grouped in religious orders, monastic warriors, secret societies, or as individual renaissance dreamers — have shared a similar vision. They imagined a global economy that empowers local economies around the world

— from the largest to the smallest — to prosper and flourish with dignity and equality, creating a global marketplace, where the spirit of Partnership and responsibility transforms emotions of anger, fear, and jealousy into passion, compassion, and empathy. Where the natural flow of information, ideas, and resources between different segments of society and across cultures transcends the unconscious exchange of baseless commodities, uniting and exalting, rather than dividing, people around the world.

The Merchant Priesthood dreamed of the rise of the Global Citizens' movement to move the world closer to their ultimate dream of a global conscious evolution. They dreamed of Global Citizens all over the world *party-cipating* through Sacred Commerce and philanthropy, creating a new world rather than fixing or changing the old one.

This spiritual vision of the future confirms the qualitative and quantitative research work of sociologist Paul H. Ray and psychologist Sherry Ruth Anderson, who documented the phenomena of the rise of the "Cultural Creative" and the Global Citizen in their book *Cultural Creatives: How 50 Million People Are Changing the World* (2000).

This "new" group of people challenged the standard paradigms: the modernist interpretation of the world — nation-state-centric, where technology and progress will solve the day, the environment is important, but security more so — and the traditional view of the world — strong patriarchy, strong religion, strong culture, and agriculturally based.

Ray and Anderson went so far as to say that up to 25% of those in OECD (Organization for Economic Cooperation and Development) nations subscribed to the spiritual/eco/

gender partnership/global governance alternative to the capitalist position.

Ray and Anderson clearly state however that Cultural Creatives or Global Citizens do not associate themselves with a political or social movement. Indeed, they represent a paradigm change in values: authenticity, holistic world approach of interconnectedness, idealism and activism, globalism and ecology, equality of men and women in business, life, and politics, altruism, self-actualization and spirituality.

Personally, in the light of what has happened in the last decade and a half, we would prefer to call these global, active, innovative citizens "Culture Creators," as we believe a whole new culture is currently being created.

Oxfam defines Global Citizens as individuals who are aware of the wider world and have a sense of their own role as a world citizen. They respect and value diversity, have an understanding of how the world works economically, politically, and socially, are outraged by social injustice, and are willing to act to make the world a more sustainable and caring place, taking full responsibility for their actions. They recognize the interdependence of all people and, through cooperative effort, they make a difference in their community and their world.

In most discussions, the Global Citizens' movement is a sociopolitical process rather than a political organization or party structure. Sometimes, the term is used synonymously with the anti-globalization movement, not that Global Citizens are against the ideal of globalization, but they know from their own experience of history that multinationals and governments in general can misuse or abuse this ideal. They are against the creation of a world government and the blending together of cultures to create a monoculture based mainly on Western ideals and unsustainable consumerism. They have decided to take action and *party-cipate*.

Some of the earliest recorded material found on the concept of a Global Citizen first emerged among the Greek Cynics in the fourth century BC, who coined the term "cosmopolitan," meaning "citizen of the world." The Roman Stoics later elaborated on the concept. The contemporary concept of cosmopolitanism, which proposes that all individuals belong to a single moral community, has gained a new salience as scholars examine the ethical requirements of this planetary phase of civilization.

Millions of humans across every important sector of business today are working for a more abundant, conscious world. Even though they may not be consciously aware, they are indeed manifesting the values of the spiritual current of the Merchant Priesthood via their practice of Conscious Living, Right Livelihood, Emotional Intelligence and *"party-cipatory* philanthropy."

Party-cipatory philanthropy is a philanthropy that is sourced in empathy rather than sympathy — and in joy rather than guilt. It is about people coming together to create change, actively participating in projects and watching them grow. *Party-cipatory* philanthropy requires individuals to take full responsibility for the direction and impact of the service or contribution they provide.

Global Citizens like Lynn Twist, author of *The Soul of Money*, add texture and a human dimension when it comes to matters of profit. Rather than calling a charitable group or service center a "non-profit," Twist renames these vital strands in the human fabric "social-profit" organizations. As she says: "There is nothing 'non' about non-profits." There is a profit; it's called "social profit." Similarly, Kevin Danaher, founder of *Global Exchange* and the *Green Festival*, uses the term "non-profit entrepreneur" to reflect the newly emerging philosophy in the world of philanthropy.

Nobel Peace Prize–winner Dr. Mohammad Yunus, founder of the microlending movement, speaks of the rate of return in broader terms than money, focusing on the number of trees planted, lives saved, families salvaged, individuals educated, and villages lifted out of poverty. Dr. Yunus would like to see a stock market evolve specifically for social-profits, allowing them to compete with each other, checking and comparing their rate of "social" and "environmental" return, thus bringing the concept of competition in its real meaning to philanthropy.

Competition, in its highest form, is about competing to bring out the best in each other, a feedback mechanism showing us where we have room for improvement and where we can congratulate ourselves for a job well done.

Crowdfunding is a prime example of one of the new *party-cipatory* opportunities. Easy, effective, fun, and exciting, it allows individuals and organizations to invest or contribute money to support people in need, creative ideas, important causes, and new businesses.

In 2012, according to the Crowdfunding Industry Report by *Massolution*, philanthropic crowdfunding supported more than one million global campaigns, raising more than $2.7 billion. The projected figures for 2014 are expected to be in the region of $5.16 billion. In the past, funds have been raised via large donations from a few wealthy donors, whereas crowdfunding organizations generate small donations from many millions of donors. In this way, we are all able to connect with the causes closest to our hearts and non-profits have the opportunity to find donations from sources worldwide. This is the democratization of philanthropy, where meaningful, collaborative participation is open to all, using creative, educational, and easy-to-access methods.

Currently, we are involved in a cultural evolution. Ours is an age of *party-cipation*. No longer are we limited to learning from gurus, teachers, and scripture. We are consciously evolving into Global Citizens, who have access to all traditions; we can pick and choose and custom-design our own unique spiritual practice and path. The spiritual hierarchy of love and support has spread and awakened consciousness throughout the species, so that we are now able to mentor one another, and ourselves, rather than rely on members of the religious community.

In Silicon Valley, the influence of these Knights of E-Commerce has moved light years beyond the work of organized sects and brotherhoods. The work and ideals of Sacred Commerce are now manifesting worldwide, at the stroke of a key, every minute, on every continent, spontaneously, through the individual work of many different people, some of whom may never meet in person.

In today's world, religious and esoteric orders are no longer needed to elevate the overall Resonance of the culture. The work is carried forward through loosely affiliated groups of like-minded people, who are connected through horizontal networks of equal relationships, rather than across the vertical chain-of-command hierarchies, typical of the traditional organizations of the past. These horizontal networks are spreading across every continent, across all genders and cultures, across all ages, classes, religions, and beliefs, throughout the world and the Web. We're witnessing the rise of the Global Citizen.

Right use of technology is more crucial now than ever before. At this time in history, our machines aspire to near-human capacities and reflect both our conscious and unconscious selves. We, as the gods of these machines, must now be clear on what manner of gods we wish to be — and on what kind of future we are intent on creating, for the machines will be sure to reflect that intent.

Over the ages, the Merchant Priests were directly or partially responsible for many of the creative enterprises that uplifted humanity and contributed to cultural evolution. Their efforts laid the foundation for a spreading global middle class and distributing the seeds of capitalism that bankrolled democracy and freedom for well over a billion people, firstly in the West and now all over the world. Yet as "Priests," their historic business success remained deeply reflective of their continued commitment to self-realization.

The spiritual current we are speaking of today is transparent, all-inclusive, and available to all. You need not take vows or wear a robe and collar to tap the pulse or be carried upstream by this gracious current. The Merchant Priesthood has passed the baton to the collective and infused the shared domain of human thought and aspiration with these ideas and values. The sacred dimension of Commerce calls to us from the future, inviting us to *party-cipate*.

The next important wake-up call alerts us to exercise care and attention, as we select the products and services we exchange. As Global Citizens with one eye scanning ahead toward our most elegant future, we shop and spend, click and send with our ear to the ground, listening for the pulsing magnetic force, the "strange attractor" that has always called us forward and required of us our best: **Beauty, Goodness, and Truth**, heralding the birth of the Sacred Consumer. It is this refined context and precise focus that allows the magic and the miracles to flow into the various avenues and enterprises we choose.

Sacred Consumers are not only conscious of what they consume and its impact on their bodies and the environment, but also how it affects their consciousness and the consciousness of others.

Many of you reading this book already see yourselves as social inventors or engineers. You are the heralds, the people bringing meaning, ethics, emotion, and caring into business, education, and government institutions. We are revolutionizing the way business gets done, the way we interact with each other, and the way we think.

As the sacred and the feminine return to our daily lives, Commerce will reveal its ultimate gift, a powerful tool for conscious evolution.

Since the time of the Merchant Priesthood in ancient Egypt, Merchant Priests (although not always known by this name) have existed throughout our history — and still exist to this day in every culture around the world. They are the renaissance men and women who dedicate their lives to working either overtly or behind the scenes to create Abundance and Prosperity, helping humanity to evolve. Their vision of a Global Citizen continues to exert its influence to this day.

The Merchant Priest is awakening in all of us. The ancients set the frame and crafted the morphic field; now we play our part, in spinning out the meme — cultural information that propagates from one mind to another.

The secret is out: *party-cipation* **in the pursuit of Beauty, Goodness, and Truth IS the blueprint for a new humanity**.

The time of tooth-and-claw struggle and martyrdom is over and the time for magic and miracles is now.

By reading this far, you have nearly completed the Merchant Priesthood initiation. What is left is for you to take the mantle. Vows of celibacy and poverty are not required. All that is required is a willingness to receive — and a desire to *party-cipate* in manifesting the dream of Prosperity, Peace, and Conscious Evolution for us all.

PART FOUR

THE SACRED JOURNEY

"... For the heroes of all time have gone before us; the labyrinth is thoroughly known; we have only to follow the thread of the hero-path. And where we had thought to find an abomination, we shall find a god; where we had thought to slay another, we shall slay ourselves; where we had thought to travel outward, we shall come to the center of our own existence; where we had thought to be alone, we shall be with all the world."

—JOSEPH CAMPBELL, *The Hero with a Thousand Faces*

THE MAGICAL HERO'S
JOURNEY

HERE WE WOULD LIKE TO SHARE WITH YOU THE BLUEPRINT OF our own Hero's Journey, influenced by the many great Hero's Journeys throughout the ages and sourced in a confluence of mythologies from around the world. Our own Journey — as with all journeys — is in a state of continuous evolution.

We invite you to use this blueprint as an open source template or a springboard to custom design your own Hero's Journey, in alignment with your own unique customs, culture, spirituality, or religion.

Throughout this book, we have used the terms "God," "Goddess," "the Divine," and "the Pulse," aware that this source of life is known by many different names. Please use the word with which you feel most comfortable. The key is that Beauty, Goodness, and Truth are found within the intrinsic core of all religions and faiths — and exist even within atheism.

On our own journey, we have discovered that we are not alone. Along the way, we have created alliances and partnerships with a multitude of friends, both seen and unseen. We have received gifts, found treasures, and reawakened the magical parts of ourselves that had lain dormant for a long time.

As with any true spiritual path, there are no set-in-stone prerequisites for the Journey. However, it is extremely valuable to have an understanding, and some experience of Emotional Intelligence, Emotional Alchemy, Resonance, and Meditation. That is why we include in this section of the book a summary of and basic training in these skills.

To go deeper, trainings, tools, and other resources are available at *SacredCommerce.com*.

EMOTIONAL ALCHEMY

THE MERCHANT PRIESTS' GREATEST SKILL AND CHALLENGE was to be able to take their inner training into the marketplace, rather than preserving it for the safe and serene environment of the temple. It is one thing to be able to hold a stable, radiant presence when protected by temple walls, but quite another to be able to sustain the Resonance of harmony and flow, while in the thick of daily transactions and emotions.

When a Merchant Priest or a modern-day Knight of Commerce steps into the marketplace — whether it be a souk in old Cairo or a board meeting in Silicon Valley — they need to be sensitive to and aware of the swirl of emotional energies that are shaping and influencing their environment.

Nothing can shake us from our center more easily than the numbers in our bank balance or affairs of the heart. In the marketplace, both of these can be simultaneously present. One person may be jealous of another; several may be absorbed in their greed; others will be speaking and acting from a sense of fear; while a couple of associates in the corner may be in the midst of some smoldering argument or the beginnings of a passionate love affair.

The Merchant Priest would have trained long and hard to be able to step into these complex environments and, by holding their own high Resonance, would be able to raise the Resonance of those around them. In this same way, the modern day counterpart of the Merchant Priest is able to not only protect himself from the forces swirling around him, but can also harmonize the energies of the group for the benefit of all and for the good of the transaction, whether it be for the sale of a pound of apples or the merger of two Fortune 500 companies.

The Merchant Priests' power was derived from their Emotional Intelligence and their understanding of Resonance.

In 1997, my partner, Dr. Robert Cooper, and I wrote a book called *Executive EQ: Emotional Intelligence in Leadership and Organizations,* where we defined Emotional Intelligence as "the ability to sense, understand, and effectively apply the power and the acumen of emotions, as a source of energy, information, and connection."

We also suggested the "Four Cornerstone Model" as a way to help executives and business leaders around the world to build and develop a new, sustainable, emotionally intelligent corporate culture.

After the book was published, many business consultants and life coaches added the term "Emotional Intelligence" to the services they offered their employees and clients. Disappointingly, however, some simply rebranded their existing psychological and personal development tools without any significant changes. It is possible that some people thought we had done the same thing — and maybe, partially, we did. However, few seemed to recognize the fact that emotions are a source of energy and information and that this is what Emotional Intelligence is all about.

What I will be sharing with you here is the summary of the Four Levels of Emotional Intelligence, as inspired by the Four Cornerstone Model.

Students in the Merchant Priesthood in ancient Egypt were trained to gain proficiency in not just one, but all **Four Levels** of **Emotional Intelligence: Emotional Literacy, Emotional Fitness, Emotional Depth**, and **Emotional Alchemy**.

The **First Level, Emotional Literacy**, means becoming literate in the language — learning the alphabet and the grammar of emotions. We define Emotional Literacy as the ability to recognize, acknowledge, and express our emotions in an appropriate way. It is about "reading" and "writing" emotions. "Reading" emotions is about empathy. It is the ability to feel someone else's feelings in that moment, while "writing" emotions is about expressing and communicating your feelings. It is vitally important that we learn to express our emotions appropriately, instead of reverting to what our friend Lazaris calls "the 4Ds" — Denying them, Defending them, Diminishing them, or Distracting from them. Our emotions are simply raw energy and data, which we can transform into power and choose to use consciously and elegantly in our daily lives.

For our purposes here, we will be working mostly with the root emotions of fear, anger, and jealousy, and the primary emotions of love and joy. Obviously, we are aware that there are many other emotions, but we believe they are all more or less derived from these root and primary emotions.

Emotions are neither negative nor positive; we prefer to call them "constricting" or "expansive." The root emotions of fear, anger, and jealousy are constricting emotions; they constrict our choices, forcing us to deal with the imperative issue at hand. The emotions of love, passion, and joy, on the other hand, are expansive emotions, as they expand or open us up to a far wider spectrum of choice. Both are needed.

The Merchant Priest understood that strong feelings such as fear, anger, and jealousy are neither "wrong" nor "bad." In fact, they are each appropriate in the right situation and have enabled the human race to survive. This is why they are hard-wired into our nervous system. If we deny or ignore these messages from the lower parts of our body, we disconnect ourselves from the vital energy and information they carry. Recognizing and harnessing these raw energies or root emotions is a far better response than allowing them to cause damage by spilling out of us unconsciously or remaining within us, creating dis-ease.

Emotional Literacy teaches us to respect the emotions broadcast from the "lower centers" — the first three Chakras in the human organism — and to pay attention to them as a personal feedback mechanism, providing valuable signals or information about what is going on in our reality. In time, we learn to see these emotions not so much as base in themselves, but rather as denser expressions of finer energies.

Woven into the very root of our being is what the yogis call the first or *root* Chakra, found at the base of the pelvis. This is what Abraham Maslow would call the survival instinct, the response that registers in consciousness as the fight, flight, or freeze mechanism. The emotion that drives this response is fear, especially the mother of all fears: the fear of death. The second or *sacral* Chakra, situated behind the navel, governs our basic need for safety and security. Anger is the driving force here. Then the third or *solar plexus* Chakra, just beneath the diaphragm, is the seat of our need for belonging and relationship. This is where jealousy thrives.

The Merchant Priests of ancient Egypt knew that both emotions and thoughts were electromagnetic energies and saw these emotions first and foremost as a source of energy, information, and attraction. In physics, "e" is the symbol of energy and therefore, emotion could be spelled "e-motion," as it is literally, "energy in motion." "E-motion" comes from the Latin *emotivus*, meaning "energy that moves within us." Scientists corroborate this by confirming that both our feelings and our thoughts are indeed electromagnetic energy.

The Merchant Priests saw emotions as morally neutral, just like electricity or magnetism; some constricting, some expansive, but none were labeled or judged "good" or "bad," "negative" or "positive." For example, if we put our finger into a live electric socket, we will receive a shock, shouting, "Ow!"; however, if we direct that current by installing a bulb and switching on the light, we may find ourselves saying, "Wow!"

Similarly, our emotions are neutral; it is the way we express them that makes them either negative or positive. If we suppress, ignore, or inappropriately express our emotions, they become negative, whereas, if we express our emotions appropriately, they become positive.

Once we have trained ourselves to feel the emotion that is arising within us, allowing us to recognize and name it, we can discover the message it carries and — exercising discernment — make an informed choice as to how we respond, according to the situation.

The Merchant Priests would welcome whatever emotion arose in them, engaging it in dialogue to discover its message. With the assistance of associated bodily sensations, they would reflect upon the emotion, examining its components and diving as deeply as they could into the felt experience, unearthing the real issues the emotion was trying to bring to their attention. The more they were able to befriend their emotions, the more conscious their feeling-self became and the easier it was to transmute the denser emotional frequencies into a finer, higher Resonance.

The Priests knew that anger, fear, and jealousy did not simply arise from nowhere, for no reason, like some arbitrary or freak thunderstorm. They were taught to receive and welcome these emotions as valuable messengers, delivering important information about their relationship with their current environment or reality.

For example, the Merchant Priest would know that anger is a signal that things are not happening the way they want them to — and they would receive it as a call to take responsibility and take action accordingly. Anger is a raw energy that wants and needs to be directed. If we fail to direct it consciously, we might end up doing some damage, which we may later regret. When anger is expressed with awareness, it lifts the energy into its higher octave of courage, enabling us to correct what went wrong and transforming it into its highest octave of passion.

Learning to harness anger, fear, and jealousy and to direct them to positive ends was a highly refined art amongst the Egyptians. Just as the Eskimos have some thirty different words for snow, and the Indians — who have made a science of the breath — have many names for various breathing patterns, the Egyptians had twenty to thirty different names for each of the root emotions.

The Egyptians were not only concerned with harnessing and directing the base emotions; the same guidelines applied to the whole emotional spectrum.

Anxiety, for example, was interpreted as a message that we need to improve our skills; it was seen as the premonition of a fear coming from the future, which, if not dealt with, would cause some kind of trouble, embarrassment, or shame. Boredom offered the message that new skills needed to be learned. Depression warned the individual of being on someone else's board game — rather than his or her own — and that, over time, emotions had been suppressed or "depressed," deep down.

Merchant Priests would harness their energies by firstly bringing them into conscious awareness. This is the foundation of Emotional Literacy — to pause, for example, when we are afraid and to notice: *My body is sending me a signal of fear.* Making the emotion of fear conscious in this way may sound simple — and in a way it is — however, it requires an intentional moment of self-reflection, which can easily be drowned out by the power of the emotion's habitual tendency to trigger an unconscious, knee-jerk response of fight, flight, or freeze.

The power and persuasiveness of the knee-jerk reaction is hardly surprising. After all, it has been programmed into us genetically for millions of years and is in our biochemistry. Although in our modern day-to-day reality, we very rarely encounter situations that are truly life-threatening, we can still all too easily succumb to our biochemistry and over-react in certain situations, responding as if we were in fact in some mortal danger.

The good news is that, more recently in our evolution, we have developed a neocortex that enables us to bypass the automatic reaction with a conscious response, one that is more appropriate to the reality of the situation we've found ourselves in. However, it is not enough to know this theoretically; we need to see and acknowledge the power of our conditioning, learn steps toward conscious intervention, and then consistently put those steps into practice.

Just as the pianist first learns the names of the keys and the differences between them, the Merchant Priest would learn to recognize the different types of emotion at his or her disposal, along with their functions. Then, as the pianist learns to gather the notes into a tune and eventually into a whole sonata, so the Merchant Priest would develop the skills and dexterity of "playing" his or her emotions to maximum effect, creating beautiful realities.

Once emotionally literate, the Priests would go about exercising their emotional muscles and develop their **Emotional Fitness,** the **Second Level** of Emotional Intelligence. With Emotional Fitness, we start to become more conscious and begin to integrate our emotions into our life skills — our character, trust, self-esteem, confidence, respect, etc. — giving them more depth and greater strength.

In our early years of exploring Emotional Intelligence, Rowan came to me one day after meditating, saying: "I've just found out that my character is wobbly." "Character," in this sense, means how frequently we adhere to our principles. For example, if one of our principles in life is to be honest — and we're not — then we lack "character."

Rowan was clearly in a state of shock, as was I. As far as I knew, she had a high sense of character and I asked her what she meant. She replied, "I don't always tell the truth. I don't lie about the facts and figures — in fact I've always prided myself on my honesty in that way — but I've just realized that I lie about how I feel. My friends ask me, 'How do you feel 'about this or that?' and I say, 'It's fine,' even when it's not. I'm so scared of the impact of my feelings, I just lie about them."

Rowan became aware that she had a lot of room to strengthen her character. By adding this element of emotional awareness, she learned to be more emotionally honest with herself and others, thereby adding breadth and strength to her character. In addition, it allowed her to trust her character more fully and to deal more successfully with a far wider range of experiences.

Let's take another example of how emotions can give depth and strength to another life skill, such as trust. Many of us have issues with trust, because we have so often felt betrayed and hurt. When considering trusting someone, we usually check with our logic, reason, and intuition, but rarely do we check in with our emotions to see if they're also on board. We thereby deprive ourselves of vital data and information. When we add our feelings to the equation, our choice to trust another or ourselves is more stable with a much higher chance of success.

By becoming emotionally fit, we move from developing "life skills" to gaining "life mastery." This is where our life starts flowing and working smoothly with loving and intimate relationships, good health, and success at work and in life. Then comes the big question: What next?

This is the stage where we are ready to enter the **Third Level** of Emotional Intelligence, called **Emotional Depth**. Emotional Depth means exploring the depth of who you are. It is in your depth that you will find your truer self, receive your gifts or grace, and discover your treasures. In your depth, you hear the voice of your soul and spirit calling you home. This is where your destiny reveals itself to you — and where your spirituality abounds. Here is where a relationship of Partnership with the Divine becomes possible, moving beyond a relationship of fear and/or love.

Imagine your Emotional Depth as a deep pool. On the surface of the pool float your lighter emotions, such as fear, anger, and jealousy. If you are unequipped, you will simply test the waters with your toe and refuse to go deeper, worried about what you will discover. However, if you are equipped with your Emotional Literacy and Fitness, you can trust yourself more fully and happily dive deeply into the pool, knowing you are perfectly capable of dealing with whatever you may encounter.

Splashing your angers, fears, and jealousies away, you may have to slay a few dragons, remnants of your negative shadow or things from your past, which you have not as yet dealt with. You can then dive deeper to the bottom of the pool, where the heavier emotions lie — your integrity, your Goodness, Beauty, magnificence, majesty, and your sense of greatness. This is where the keys to your spirituality await you.

Once your gifts are received and your treasures discovered, you emerge from the pool of your emotions with access to huge reserves of previously untapped power.

Having integrated all of the different aspects of Self and developed a truly authentic presence, the modern-day Merchant Priest who reaches this level acts from a core of fundamental integrity. Integrity's main function is to create the space for all different aspects of Self to come together without judgment and to work together as one.

The modern-day Merchant Priest's presence and actions come from an inner stillness and confidence, which is the root of their authority and leadership that those around them can feel and resonate with. This is where leadership becomes a love affair between the leader and those whom he or she leads.

This level of attainment is an indication that we have reached the **Fourth Level** of Emotional Intelligence, which we call **Emotional Alchemy**. Here, we are on the accelerated slope, beginning to actively, consciously create our futures, where we achieve a rarefied state of intuitive flow and spiritual self-mastery.

When writing the book *Executive EQ,*, Dr. Robert Cooper and I wondered if a phrase like "Emotional Alchemy" would land like a foreign tongue on the ears of a corporate world, where reason was the primary language. In the early 1990s, alchemy of any kind was too far-fetched for some and too esoteric for others. Although we knew that including such a concept was a risk, we followed our intuition and went with it. More than two decades have passed since *Executive EQ* was first published and its success has more than validated the wisdom of that risk. In 2002, we were pleased to see Tara Bennett-Goleman release a book entitled *Emotional Alchemy*, which was similarly well received across a wide and willing readership.

From studies of the brain, scientists have proven that when we feel an emotion, the brain secretes certain hormones and chemicals — and that each emotion has a different "chemical signature." Therefore, when emotions are mixed together, they produce different chemicals and simultaneously produce an alchemical reaction within us.

Learning Emotional Alchemy is rather like a trainee chemist learning the table of elements, where he or she learns that *H* is for hydrogen, *He* is for helium, *O* for oxygen, and so on. Knowing the properties of the different elements enables the trainee to use them in combination to get the desired reaction in their test tube. In the same way, a student of Emotional Alchemy must learn the effects of different emotions and their combinations, so as to avoid an explosion in the laboratory of the body-mind.

This is why we need to always be conscious and vigilant about what is happening inside of us and be aware of the emotions we are dealing with, not leaving them unattended.

The subject of Emotional Alchemy is clearly a lifelong learning experience. Since our own early explorations, Rowan and I have spent a further twenty years discovering the hidden mysteries of this subject. Our practice and experience with EQ, combined with our in-depth learning about Resonance and the quantum world, allow us now to articulate its principles to an even higher degree than before.

The word "alchemy" comes from the Arabic *al chimia,* which in the early Middle Ages simply meant "chemistry." A growing interest in the material world and its material formation, along with the budding science of chemistry, were introduced into Europe via the Muslim Moors, who ruled southern Spain at that time. In the eleventh and twelfth centuries, the cities of Granada and Cordoba were Europe's greatest centers of civilization, attracting scholars, mystics, and merchants from three of the major religious persuasions: Judaism, Islam, and Christianity. These cities were themselves a sort of alchemical distillation vessel, in which different strands of esoteric knowledge were combined to create fresh and visionary insights into the potential of human nature.

Until that time, Western civilization had been entirely absorbed in the story of Christianity and the culture as a whole had eyes only for religious practices and the afterlife. The material world was considered a vale of tears, something to pass through as quickly as possible, in order to reach the "real" life, which lay beyond death. However, in southern Spain at this time, new interests and new ways of thinking began to take root, which gave value to the world of matter as well as to the world of spirit.

It was in this atmosphere that the interest in chemistry and the science of matter began to grow. And it was here too that the meaning of alchemy, as we use the word today, began to emerge, involving the study of how it might be possible to refine the energies in the human being to the point where they miraculously transform into spiritual energies. Far from trying to escape the body and its denser energies for some rarified spiritual realm, these explorers saw the material world and the human body as the raw materials for their own spiritual transformation.

While there were certainly many who interpreted this transformative, alchemical ideal in a literal sense — of the quest to turn a base metal like lead into pure gold — the true alchemists saw their own human body and mind as the real laboratory. For them, the raw materials for their experiments were their emotions.

The Emotional Alchemist understands the basic tenets of chemistry and applies them to the emotional realm. The chemical reaction that occurs when two hydrogen atoms combine with one oxygen atom to make water is well understood by any student of high school chemistry. What is not so well understood is that a similar natural reaction occurs in our own human biochemistry. The Merchant Priests understood this and used their knowledge to influence and leverage human emotion. For example, they could turn anger into courage by applying a specific alchemical operation. Far more than a strategy to manage or manipulate emotions, this alchemical treatment is actually an invocation that creates magic.

The treatment is so simple and elegant that you can test it out and put it to good use immediately. Although there are many nuances and levels of Emotional Alchemy, there is one "pocket remedy" that we will share with you here that you can use to transform a situation in an instant. The Merchant Priests called this basic operation "adding a drop of joy."

As we've said, every emotion has a specific chemical signature; this is called "biochemistry." Our brain and our endocrine glands secrete distinct hormones with every emotional state. For example, a flash of anger is a spray of hormonal drops, sent throughout our physiological system.

Anger alone is just as likely to provoke an act of courage, as much as an act of impulsive retaliation or an attack that would later be regretted. What the Merchant Priests of ancient Egypt understood — and this is key — is really quite elegant and simple: they understood the value of joy as a catalyst in refining and transmuting emotions. By *adding a drop of joy* to anger, an alchemical reaction occurs, transforming anger into courage. Courage is the ability to act to correct an injustice, even if we do not have all the answers yet. It is the willingness to be wrong in the pursuit of what is right.

How do we *add a drop of joy*? The best way is to truly feel it, which is easiest when we are emotionally literate and emotionally fit. However, we can also learn to conjure joy at will by calling on the memory of joy. Consider this: your brain does not know the difference between an event that is actually occurring in the moment and an event that is occurring in your imagination. When you remember and relive a joyful moment, your body will automatically re-create the chemistry of that experience.

One of my favorite ways of conjuring joy is bringing to mind the day our publisher for *Executive EQ* proposed an unusually large offer for a business book. I remember jumping up and down on my bed in sheer joy. Every time I call up that memory in order to intentionally conjure up the feeling of joy, the extreme delight of that moment readily returns to my body and mind. When I return to the matter at hand, the joy I have re-created sprinkles its biochemical hormonal "juice" over the situation. Not only have my biochemistry and perspective changed, my options for handling the situation have also become far more varied and expansive. This technique can be used in all areas of our lives, whenever a joyful boost is needed.

Let us look at an example, where we add a drop of joy to fear. Fear is a signal that something in our world needs attention. When there is cause for concern, there is a fear response in the body. Seen in this light, fear is a positive emotion, one that can guide us to act with wisdom on behalf of the people, places, and things we care about most.

Imagine for a moment that your college-bound son decides he wants to cut down on his fossil fuel use by riding a motorcycle instead of driving his gas-guzzling pickup truck. You are afraid for him and that fear has not only kept you from sleeping well for several nights, it has also been at the root of many arguments within the family.

So, you close your eyes and using your imagination, you *add a drop of joy* to your fear, by remembering the day he burst through the front door and told you he had won the school election and was now president of his class. (It's not absolutely necessary to use a memory of joy associated with the person involved. You can choose any memory that conjures up the feeling of joy at the time it is needed.) Your body responds by adding the chemistry of that joy to the chemistry of fear about your son buying a motorcycle. This allows your mind to let go of the urge to control your son and, instead, your mind becomes more spacious and the fear moves to concern. You also feel compassion and admire his attempt to make an environmentally conscious choice.

With this biochemical boost, you can now see the situation from an expanded viewpoint, making it easier to problem-solve in a creative spirit. You ask your son to look into a motorcycle safety course and you agree to go shopping together to choose the best helmet and protective clothing.

Similarly, it is possible to transmute jealousy and lift it to a higher octave. At the most basic level, jealousy is an issue of ownership. The "green-eyed monster" appears when the questions arise: *Is this mine or not? Will the love I cherish be taken away?* If yes, we get busy defending what is ours. In the best-case scenario, we become the champion and claim what is ours with honor, dignity, and respect for all concerned. In the worst-case scenario, if we haven't achieved sufficient emotional maturity to recognize jealousy for what it is, it can spiral down into envy or rage.

We have the option to talk to the "green-eyed monster" and reason with it. If we determine that what we feel jealous about does not belong to us, the next step becomes obvious. We lift jealousy to the discipline of not taking what is not ours, thereby letting go of the feeling. However, we can recognize that our jealousy has shown us something that we desire in life. By adding "one drop of joy" to that awareness, we are lifted to the ability to receive what is truly ours, from where we can experience grace.

The Merchant Priests of old Egypt knew how to close their eyes and conjure emotions at will, so as to be able to use them as raw energy. Mastery at this level gives one unique powers. This is neither self-control nor mind control nor any kind of control; this is alchemy of the highest order. Like the alchemists who turned base metals into gold, the Merchant Priests learned to turn constricting emotions into the golden opportunities that are passion, compassion, and grace. Understanding emotions as a source of energy and information, the Emotional Alchemist can lift that energy to a higher octave.

Sometimes, when I am in the last stages of completing a project, I can run out of the passion needed to finish it. The clock is ticking and deadlines are fast approaching. Sitting in meditation, I allow myself to feel the anger related to the situation for a minute or so, until enough anger hormones are released into my body-mind chamber. Then, I simply

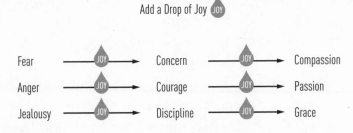

Add a Drop of Joy

conjure up a memory of joy and allow the joy "juices" to mix with the anger "juices," resulting in a sense of courage and passion, giving me the fuel needed to finish my project.

Now let's imagine someone who feels intense jealousy while in a state of extreme anger, and consider what happens if that person doesn't have the tools to process, express, and transform that anger and jealousy consciously. The resulting alchemical reactions of the anger and jealousy "juices" mixing together would create a Resonance from which feelings of envy, rage, or a desire for revenge can emerge, leading to repercussions the person may live to seriously regret.

It's important to note here the difference between joy and happiness. Happiness arises when we satisfy our needs, which Maslow lists as a hierarchy going from survival through security, relationships, and self-esteem, all the way to Beauty and spirituality. The meeting of each of these needs creates happiness. Joy, on the other hand, occurs when our *preferences* are met. Preferences are things we *like* or *enjoy* doing versus things we *need* to do.

Watching TV, going to a concert, or having sex are all preferences — something we like to do. For example, the big advance for my first book did not meet my needs of survival, security, or belonging; however, it did line up with my preferences, which were to have impact and share the concept of Emotional Intelligence with as many people as possible. I liked the idea of having the book out there. It was my preference. It lifted me into a state of joy.

Sadly, our society does not encourage us to be joyful and to do the things we prefer, as much as it promotes happiness and meeting our needs. Recently, I saw a hilarious cartoon on Facebook that illustrates this; it featured Donald Duck, saying: "Damn. Everything I like to do is either immoral, illegal, expensive, fattening, addictive, or impossible!"

The pursuit of joy is something that has become very convoluted in our society — hence so many of the things that bring us joy are in some way considered to be illegal or immoral. This is

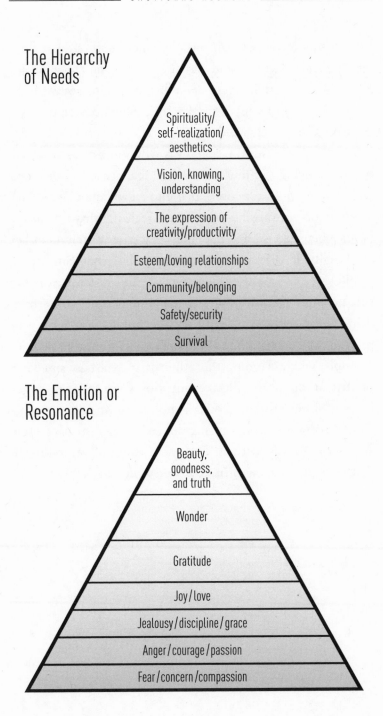

The Hierarchy of Needs

- Spirituality/ self-realization/ aesthetics
- Vision, knowing, understanding
- The expression of creativity/productivity
- Esteem/loving relationships
- Community/belonging
- Safety/security
- Survival

The Emotion or Resonance

- Beauty, goodness, and truth
- Wonder
- Gratitude
- Joy/love
- Jealousy/discipline/grace
- Anger/courage/passion
- Fear/concern/compassion

partially as a result of judgments, stemming from our parenting, religion, and society — and partially because the energy of joy is simply so powerful, we are often ill-equipped to deal with it.

For many of us, joy is used as a numbing device to cover the pain in our lives, avoiding, ignoring, and escaping the very issues we most need to face. This is why some of us are afraid of experiencing too much joy, as the feelings are so delicious and intense, we fear it could turn into an addiction. We therefore withdraw from the pursuit, not realizing that it is in the balance between joy and happiness that true contentment lies.

Finally, it is important to remember that Emotional Intelligence can be used negatively. Politicians, for example, can be highly emotionally intelligent people, sometimes using their skills to manipulate the public into voting or reacting in a certain way. They can create a sense of fear, for example, when claiming the other party will raise our taxes or that immigrants will take our jobs. Or a sense of anger, when claiming that this or that politician or party are corrupt, misappropriating our tax dollars or plain stealing them and getting away with it. The main thing to remember is that ***true EQ is sourced in Love and Empathy***.

RESONANCE

THE GREATEST TOOL OF THE EMOTIONAL ALCHEMIST IS
Resonance; it is also our greatest responsibility as humans.

Quantum physics reveals that particles — light vibrat-
ing at different frequencies — are *everywhere*. When these
particles come together, they create a synergy — a standing
wave or Resonance — far more powerful than the total sum
of its parts.

Scientific breakthroughs that vastly expand our understanding of the universe are bringing with them a whole
new view of how reality functions. Notions such as "I create
my own reality, 100%" and "the law of attraction," which
may once have been suspect and readily dismissed as so
much metaphysical mumbo-jumbo, can now be verified by
leading-edge science. Ideas like alchemy can also now be
brought out of the shadow lands of the arcane and into the
realm of the good, the true (i.e., scientifically verifiable), and
the beautiful.

More and more, the existence of subtle energies and
their responsiveness to our thoughts is being verified by
experiments in quantum physics. Concepts like Resonance
are no longer the exclusive language of metaphysicians, nor
can they be dismissed as "New Age drivel."

In schools, even to this day, Newtonian physics is still
being taught, despite the fact that scientists such as Albert

Einstein, Niels Bohr, and Max Planck have proven that some aspects have been outdated for many decades. This means that many of us have been living our lives based on partial truths and false beliefs.

Einstein revealed to us that everything within our universe is pure energy, plus he explained the theory of particles. Bohr refined this, by proving the particles were actually waves, which literally changed according to who was looking at them and the person's belief system and thoughts. It was later discovered that the particles/waves, when split or separated, communicate with each other immediately, with zero regard to time and space as we experience them.

These discoveries mean that the events, conditions, and circumstances that make up our reality take shape as we expect or believe they will.

Everything we want to create exists as a wave in the quantum field, simply waiting for us to make it real. This means — based on our current understanding — that we all create everything in every aspect of our lives. If there is an element in your life that you don't like, it is entirely within your power to change it. Change your Resonance and your reality changes.

Reality precipitates or collapses, as they say in quantum physics, from your personal Resonance, which is a synergy of many different energies and frequencies, most importantly, your beliefs, feelings, thoughts, and choices. As you throw out your "hooks" — meaning your intentions, your expectations, and your imagination — into the future to draw down what you want in your life, they pass through your Resonance or, as others might call it, your "filter" or "lens."

Your filter contains the constituents of your Resonance. Any negative beliefs, thoughts, and feelings about what you want will block or diminish your desired result or goal. This is why it is important to clear your Resonance and harmonize it with what you want to manifest. This is what the Merchant Priests called "Inner Commerce," the commerce between you and your Resonance and the intention to lift it to a higher state of vibration or frequency.

Continually sharpening our hooks — of intention, expectation, and imagination — is as essential as regularly clearing our "filter" or Resonance. A lot of the time, we are told "not to expect too much or you'll be disappointed"; "don't daydream or imagine, as you'll have your hopes dashed and you'll get hurt and be upset. Better to expect nothing and then you will be neither frustrated nor disillusioned with your life." However, in the light of the concept of Resonance causation, this is a self-defeating belief system. You can get exactly what you ask for in all aspects of your life.

When training a football team, the manager would never tell the players not to expect to win or win big. On the contrary, they raise the players' expectations, constantly pumping them with the intention and desire to win and visualizations of goals scored and the crowd showering them with gratitude and love.

Today, the principles of the quantum world and the secrets of alchemy are in the public domain and we can now speak of these matters freely.

To further understand the notion of Resonance in a practical way, let us take a look at two examples: the resonance of "love" and the resonance of the "sacred."

Love itself holds a specific resonance. Inside love, there are many frequencies, such as trust, giving, respect, intimacy, caring, security, pleasure, responding, and knowing, to name a few. All these particles/frequencies come together to create the Resonance we call love.

Our personal and unique experience of love will be colored by the lens or filter through which we observe it and by the particular group of particles that make up the standing wave of our personal definition of — or belief about — love.

The Resonance of love you personally create will be made up of your unique list of ingredients, comprising all of your beliefs, thoughts, feelings, and choices about love, all of which exist as different frequencies coming together. One negates another, one adds to another, one combines with another, creating a standing wave or Resonance. Once the wave collapses into reality, you find yourself in a love affair that has your precise list of ingredients in your love-stew: your personalized, unique signature of love.

If, for example, your Resonance of love includes the belief "love hurts," or if love includes "being humiliated," then when that Resonance of love manifests into your reality, it will have that precise flavor. You have created the love affair that exactly matches your thoughts, feelings, beliefs, and choices.

How do we change our Resonance to create a different reality, if we are not happy with what we currently have in our lives? We look at all the various constituents that make up the particular Resonance we want to change and we work on releasing those aspects, which are preventing the Resonance from being the highest it can be. If we have developed a habit of associating love with pain or betrayal, for example, we work to change our thoughts and belief system and heal our emotions, so that our Resonance is free from those limiting perspectives and becomes one of success in love.

"Sacred" is also a Resonance. When we visit a sacred site, for example, Machu Picchu, a stone circle, an ancient temple, or a church, we sense the Resonance of the "sacred." Our hearts and souls are filled with the high frequencies or qualities of: Beauty, Love, Enchantment, and Mystery.

In a temple, the site might be in ruins, but we will still feel all the frequencies of Beauty (peace, joy, stillness, wonder, etc.). The colors of the scriptures and icons may be faded, the paint peeling, the walls chipped and pitted, and the wood decaying, but the core inner Beauty of this sacred place flows into our soul. As we wander through the ruins, our heart opens and we feel love, we feel enchanted. The root of the word "enchantment" is "chant" — OR "song." We hear the call of God/Goddess calling us home. We feel our soul and spirit awaken. We are drawn to the spiritual and there is a sense of mystery and the unknown. We find ourselves intrigued about what went on there, sensing the echoes of an elusive spiritual truth just beyond our reach. When these four energies — Beauty, Love, Enchantment, and Mystery — unite, they create the feeling — or Resonance — of the sacred. In this context, a "Sacred Commerce" is a Commerce that is infused with love, is enchanting, awakening our spirituality, and imbued with Beauty and a sense of mystery.

All this is moving us toward an energy perspective, one that is oriented more toward drawing in our future than concerning ourselves with our past. Western psychology asserts that the memory of a past event lives on in the present and can determine the quality of our everyday experience. This is a dimension of reality governed by the law of cause and effect. Of course, it is a valid perspective, but it is not the entire picture. An alternative perspective on reality is the concept of the future as the greatest influence determining our present reality, against the backdrop of the past.

In this way, it is possible to visualize and align ourselves with the highest possibility that our future may hold, and with that possibility, attract it to the present with our Resonance. In this way, when we learn to hold an optimistic vibration of grand possibilities of the future, we are actually drawing our future toward us, by living out the vision and frequency we hold of it in the present. This is magnetism — or — the law of attraction. In this way, *the effect becomes the cause.*

Another way the law of attraction works is in the area of health. When we have constricting emotions left unattended, they tend to come together as a Resonance stronger than the sum of all its parts, creating a receptacle or attractor for certain viruses or even accidents to come our way. Inadvertently, we have created the perfect petri dish — or Resonance — to attract that particular malady. Healing happens when one or more of the components of the Resonance is eliminated, thus changing the Resonance and robbing the illness of its environment, allowing a different Resonance to form and a different reality to manifest. When looked at like this, illnesses are far quicker to heal and the healings are often magical. When we change our personal, mental, and emotional soup —or Resonance — we create a whole new reality.

Lastly, let us look at what can happen when we are working with another person, who shares an understanding of Resonance. Rowan and I call this practice "holding the Resonance" and it is the cornerstone and primary vow of our marriage.

With pairs or groups of people, when one person is down, the other(s) tends to go down to meet them. Too often, this results in two or more individuals being down and getting stuck. A clear way to avert this pattern becomes obvious, when we look at the dynamic from an energetic perspective.

Keep in mind what we know about Resonance. When two frequencies meet, one of three things happen: the lower one comes up, the higher goes down, or they meet in the middle.

In the context of our relationship, when one of us feels down or is in a state of low Resonance for some reason — be it tiredness, illness, stress, or any of life's ever-arising challenges — the other takes a stand, "holding or raising their Resonance" to lift the other out of their funk. As opposed to feeling sad or sympathetic or being sucked into their lower Resonance, they infuse the other's Resonance with joy, happiness, hope, and compassion, as well as helping them deal with their concern and reduce their stress levels. In this way, one of us lifts the other to a higher Resonance, as if with a magnet.

Perhaps the best example of this can be seen in the case of a woman named Shelley Yates. She and her son nearly drowned after their car hydroplaned off the road and sank to the bottom of a flooded marsh. When the boy was brought to the hospital, doctors declared him brain-dead with non-viable organs and 1% chance of survival. The boy's mother, having just had a near-death experience herself, was in a kind of altered state with heightened awareness and sensitivity. She knew that if she could hold the Resonance in her son's room high enough, it could save his life. As soon as she could, she rallied everyone she knew to hold a vigil at his bedside. For twenty minutes each, one person at a time, they shared their energy field with the boy, holding a healing intent. The mother also instructed the doctors not to talk about any of the possible negative outcomes in her son's presence, rather to talk to her in the hallway. Seventy-two hours later, he opened his eyes and recognized his mother. Today, even his lingering memory problems have healed.

When we have developed the neural circuitry of an Emotional Alchemist, a true relationship of Partnership with the Divine becomes possible and, once established, gives us the unique ability to co-create reality. We cease to operate within a "cause and effect" perspective and begin to "create" by resonating with magical and elegant future realities that we *choose* to attract. In this way, as we said earlier, *the effect becomes the cause.*

When we begin to operate with the intention of creating positive realities for ourselves, *as well as for all those within our sphere of influence,* the balance of power shifts in our favor. As universal forces coalesce and realign to support our intent, we become aligned to what we call "the Pulse."

The abiding vision and hope of the Merchant Priests was that the Global Citizens, working in Partnership with the Pulse, would collectively use their wisdom and knowledge of Emotional Alchemy and Resonance to create a new world.

Let us take the concept of Resonance causation further to a global perspective and consider what we, as individuals, are collectively creating as a global reality with our cumulative Resonance.

Our media in all its formats, our government representatives, advertising, movies, video games, and individuals everywhere are contributing to the continuous dumping of negativity into our global Resonance. What sort of a world would we expect out of it?

It will have to match and comply with that Resonance. It would appear to be predominantly one of negativity — of hardship, dysfunction, struggle, war, violence, and aggression, filled with disease, poverty, interracial tension, and unsustainable use of essential resources, where our survival as a species is under threat.

That's why the Merchant Priests highly valued Inner Commerce, which, as we mentioned earlier, is the Commerce between you and the constituents of your Resonance; made up of your emotions, your beliefs, thoughts, choices, decisions, etc.

They saw Inner Commerce as the key to healing and lifting Resonance, which is the highest responsibility we have as humans on this planet.

By changing and raising our personal Resonance, we are not only changing our own reality, we are also influencing those around us, raising their Resonance and creating a domino or viral effect, simultaneously making a significant contribution toward changing and raising the global Resonance.

This is how we create a new world. A world where we move beyond hating, blaming, and attacking each other, beyond personal despair, depression, and desperation, and consciously revealing a world that resonates with Beauty, Goodness, and Truth. When these qualities enter the collective Resonance, a new Resonance is formed from which a different reality is created.

CREATING ALLIANCES WITH YOUR
_____ ROOT EMOTIONS _____

THE FIRST THREE STEPS ON THE SACRED HERO'S JOURNEY
involve creating an alliance with each of the three root
emotions: Fear, Anger, and Jealousy. Potentially, each of them
can become a strong ally who will walk alongside of you
every step of the way. Whatever challenges you face, you will
know you are not alone. Personally, I see each one of them
as my protectors and guides, offering me vital security and
wisdom on my journey.

Creating an alliance with your root emotions assumes
you are Emotionally Literate, Fit, have Depth, and understand the basics of Emotional Alchemy. You are now able to
deal with your emotions as they happen — or soon after
— gaining energy and information from them and ensuring they do not contaminate your Resonance. Making your
root emotions into allies moves the emotions beyond being
a source of energy, information, and magnetism.

Although an alliance with the emotions can be achieved
in a myriad of different ways, I would like to share with you
two highly effective methods I have used in my own life.

The first method involves personifying the emotion; i.e.
imagining it as a person. In my experience, it's much easier to

communicate with an emotion — or an energy — when it is personified; after all, we are all used to dealing with people.

This technique is not so far-fetched as it might sound, when we remember that it is also used in the field of art therapy. When, for example, a therapist would like a child to express his feelings, she may ask him to draw or personify his emotions.

If you think about it, before you create an alliance with anyone in your life, you need to have a relationship with that person, building trust and intimacy — and this method involves an identical process. By imagining your emotions as people and communicating with them as such, you begin to build a relationship, which you can later develop into a truly powerful alliance.

By personifying my own personal versions of fear, anger, and jealousy in my meditation practice, I am able to meet with them as people in my mind's eye. Having practiced this technique for some time, I now know exactly how they look and how they dress; I see their eyes, their hair, their bodies, and I know what their voices sound like, etc. Obviously, I am fully aware that they are energies — or emotions — and not real people, but by personifying them, I find it much easier to make a connection.

When you begin this process, dismiss any concerns you might have about feeling silly or worrying about how long the process might take. No two people will see, hear, sense, or experience their emotions in the same way. We are all unique individuals and there is absolutely no set experience or result to be anticipated, so feel at ease and approach this practice with an open, relaxed mind. There is no time pressure; you may get a response immediately or it may take a while. All that is needed is practice, perseverance, and patience — and your own unique alliance will be created.

In the beginning, you might not see anyone, but you may be able to feel or sense their presence. For example, in the beginning you might sense that your anger is strong or weak, muzzled or sadistic, chained deep within you or running freely without boundaries. Endeavor to make no judgments. Just be aware and accept the state of your emotion, exactly as it appears at this time, making it feel comfortable and at ease, understanding it is simultaneously intrigued and wary, just as you are. At this stage, you are simply getting to know one another — and getting to know yourself.

As you allow your anger to reveal itself, you will be able to engage in conversation with it, just like talking with a friend or a partner, which is exactly what it has the potential to be. At first, you may have to imagine the personified emotion's responses in order to catalyze the process of dialogue. In time, with practice, you will begin to hear it speak for itself in response to you.

When you start hearing yourself saying, "What a great idea, I never would have thought of that," or something of the kind, hinting that there is someone else with you or communicating with you, then you will know you are in alliance with your emotions. At this stage, your emotions are upgraded from being a messenger and source of energy, to being an ally providing you with invaluable advice and support, answers, or a solution to a question or issue. With time and patience, you will develop a strong, reliable alliance based on trust.

To create an alliance with fear and jealousy, you follow exactly the same process. Once your alliances have become established, these emotions can be called upon and consulted whenever you need some advice or need to make a choice or decision.

For myself, I imagine a round table, where we all meet to discuss any issues I might have. On a regular basis, we sit together and I share my plans with them, requesting advice and feedback. I see my emotions as my advisors or my inner board of directors; each of them is an honored friend and trusted ally.

When Dr. Robert Cooper and I were working on the book *Executive EQ,* for example, the time came to decide on whose name should appear first on the cover and I became aware of some inner turmoil. Although the idea for the book was mine and Dr. Cooper had been initially hired as a researcher, we had both developed the concept of *Executive EQ* and, as we worked so well together, we had become partners. However, I realized there was an issue simmering within me, concerning personal recognition. My business sense told me that Dr. Cooper's name should be first on the cover; whereas I was an engineer and an entrepreneur, he had written many successful business books, had a PhD in Psychology, and was well known in the business community. However, my ego wanted recognition, saying: "This is my project; this is my work."

In meditation, I sat with my emotions and asked them: "Guys, what do you think? Whose name should be first, his or mine?" Both Anger and Fear said nothing, but Jealousy, which I rarely hear from, had something to say and I asked: "What's your concern, Jealousy?" It replied: "Well, if Dr. Cooper's name is first, people might think that he is the primary initiating author. You might feel a bit jealous and then you might start sabotaging the project. Every time you give the book to someone and they look at it and they see 'Dr. Robert Cooper and Ayman Sawaf,' you will find yourself saying, 'And by the way, this was my project, I hired Dr. Robert Cooper to do this...' along with other egocentric responses. And this, in time, might undermine and sabotage the project, because you will be diminishing his value and his contribution, giving power to your negative ego and allowing it to mess up the Resonance." I then asked: "What shall I do, Jealousy?" and the reply came: "Just have a statement in the preface saying how the book came about, acknowledging and honoring your personal contribution." In this way, Jealousy gave me an effective, acceptable solution.

When *Executive EQ* was later published in Holland, I received a copy of the book and I saw immediately that Dr. Cooper's name on the front cover was not only first, but also in huge print, whereas my own was second and in very small print. My initial instinctive response was one of jealousy. My first thought was to call the publisher, requesting him to withdraw the Dutch edition and to reprint the book, creating all sorts of problems. That was until I remembered to take a look at the preface. There I found the acknowledgement of my contribution to the project and I smiled, feeling instantly soothed and thanking Jealousy for its vital input.

The second method I use to create an alliance with my emotions is seeing them as a mirror. When I experience a situation that triggers intense emotion within me, I interpret it as a hint or guidance or a message that there is something there for me to examine. It is pointing out to me that this situation mirrors something in me that I need to work on.

Let me share with you another personal example. A few years ago, one particular world leader would regularly appear on the news. He made me so angry, I wanted to punch the television set! Reflecting on this reaction, my alliance with Anger showed me: "There is something here that reflects — or mirrors — something inside of you. Take a look." When I explored this, acknowledging that I create my own reality 100% and therefore I have created that particular leader for a specific reason, I asked myself: "What does this person represent *to* me? What does he represent *in* me? What is this world leader *mirroring* in me?" The answer? Leadership.

In my meditation practice, I then explored my own leadership qualities and I was appalled by what I discovered. I found my leadership skills to be shallow, with little follow-through; they were fragile, they messed up a lot, and they clearly needed to be improved. I thought leadership was simply telling people what to do — especially being the owner of the company — instead of inspiring my employees by my example. I also remembered how many times people had pointed this out to me and how many times I'd ignored them.

Over time, I reviewed all of my businesses and my leadership of the various teams and I realized that my leadership qualities and skills needed to improve dramatically.

In this instance, my trusted ally, Anger, had clearly directed me toward a mirror I needed to look into, pinpointing something in need of healing or improving. Over time I have discovered that on almost every occasion, Fear, Anger, and Jealousy have proven to be wise and trusted allies.

Another way to pinpoint what is being mirrored back to you — beyond awareness of how intense or moderate the emotion is — is by noticing how close a certain reality is to you.

Let me share another personal example to explain what I mean. When I'm watching the news, if I see people experiencing survival issues, such as dying from hunger on another continent, although I may feel for them and feel their pain, I am also aware that it is far removed from my own life. It is still, however, in my reality. I am creating it — by either causing it or allowing it to happen — and thus, I still need to take responsibility. This could mean I close my eyes and pray for them or put them in a white light or send a contribution to a relevant charity to support them. However, if an issue of poverty or survival is in my village or in my family, this is much closer to me and I need to take this more seriously. It is an indicator that survival is an issue I need to examine in more depth.

In this way, our allies are always pinpointing areas we need to explore within ourselves or for which we need to take greater responsibility.

Once this alliance with our root emotions has been created and we have the benefit of three powerful, trustworthy allies walking by our side, we are ready to move on to the next step, which is creating a Partnership with the Pulse.

PARTNERSHIP WITH
THE PULSE

ALTHOUGH A RELATIONSHIP WITH "THE PULSE" — THAT ultimate resonant energy of the universe — is available for all of us at all times, a *partnership* can really only be achieved once a certain level of emotional maturity has been attained.

While emotions and the associated matrix of psychological forces are an essential foundation of our existence, we humans are also spiritual beings.

At this stage of our journey, we leave behind our child-like connection to God that pleads, "*Help me with this, God. Will you do it for me, please? Please might I have a miracle?*" We are no longer in servitude to the "Powers-That-Be," we come well versed in the language of relationship, and are equipped with our passion, compassion, and our ability to receive. We know how to transmute energy with joy and create magical realities with Emotional Alchemy.

This energy — the Pulse — resonates across a graduated spectrum of forces, all the way up to the Infinite Source, known by any of a thousand names. As such, the highest wisdom is available to those with the ability to tune in to this energy. The quality and quantity of wisdom available exists in proportion to our sensitivity to the Pulse and our degree of attunement.

In our lives, we may often become lost in the wilderness, but sooner or later, we all once again resonate with the Pulse, where we are reunited with her divine energy.

Once our core Partnership with the Pulse has been established, true miracles can really happen. To establish our Partnership, we use the fuel of our passion and enthusiasm, along with the skill of generating the correct Resonance. Passion is the router connecting us to the entire Web of Creation. It is the force for the good and the true that enables our sense of interconnectedness and joy.

The Greek root of the word "enthusiasm" means "being filled or infused with the breath of God." This is why the quality of enthusiasm has always been so highly prized. It is a natural expression of the individual soul, a hint of the divinity bestowed on each of us.

In its higher octave, enthusiasm turns to joy. Joy is the spontaneous expression of the human spirit. The more fully we engage in our lives and dive into our days without resistance, the more our joy will burst forth and infect everyone around with delight for our common purpose, whatever it may be. The more joy we have in our life, the more we know that our life is not ours alone; rather, joy is a co-creation with its own inherent purpose and spirit.

Our ability to attune to the Pulse is also directly related to the level of commitment we bring to the matter of *self-responsibility*. Most of us have spent years engaging in personal growth and conscious evolution — and recognize this level of self-responsibility. If, for example, we find an ingredient in our love relationship that we do not like, we don't blame or point fingers, we get busy unearthing our core beliefs and attitudes and make the changes at that level.

If we have been diligent in our personal evolution, we may even be at the stage a Merchant Priest reached later in life, where the root emotions — fear, anger, and jealousy — automatically transmute into higher frequencies, because they occur within an ocean of joy.

Everything that exists emanates from a spectrum of frequencies which, taken together, form a particular energy signature or Resonance. As we become sensitive to our own particular Resonance, we can begin to consciously act in tune with it.

In the process of exploring my own Resonance and becoming more conscious of its different components, I have found the expansive frequencies of love, courage, curiosity, enthusiasm, joy, fun, and the willingness to have impact — alongside the more constricting frequencies of needing to be in control, perfection, arrogance, and judgment — all mixing together to create the person I am.

In my own spiritual growth, as I consciously take out and heal the constricting emotions and add the balancing frequencies of peace, stillness, and humility, a whole new Resonance is being shaped. An alchemical reaction — or a metamorphosis — happens and a more beautiful me is created. This is something I do again and again and again.

Constricting emotions do not go away. When I am under stress, they raise their heads once again — and each and every time, I can choose how to respond to them and can take the necessary steps to raise my personal Resonance.

The Pulse has certain qualities — Beauty, Goodness, and Truth are primary among them — and, as we cultivate these qualities, we learn how to develop them and then project their Resonance into our everyday lives. The Pulse also contains the blueprint of our possible future and destiny and as we bring its unique Resonance into our daily existence, we literally draw our future to us in the here and now.

When we align ourselves with the Pulse in this way, we enter the realm of miracles. Magic is a shift in perspective that allows us to see what wasn't there a moment ago. Any magician knows the importance of perspective to his craft, for it is perspective that lends magic to every sleight of hand. When we create magic by consciously changing our Resonance, for example, we apply a sort of inner sleight of hand to our current reality. This is the magic that opens the window to unseen possibilities, showing us how it can shift our reality.

Consciously creating miracles is of another order altogether and this is where a Partnership with the Pulse is essential. Miracles are events that happen without effort, which turn out better than we could ever have desired, expected, or imagined. They are the result of co-creation with the Divine; they typically startle us, because they seem to come out of nowhere.

Through co-creation with the Pulse, a synergy is generated that achieves results far greater than the sum of its parts, though this can only happen if we come to the Partnership emotionally clear.

There are only two rules that come with this co-creation. Firstly, our success is always shared, acknowledging the role played by our partner. Secondly, if for any reason our venture does not live up to our expectations, we must take full responsibility for any shortcomings ourselves, knowing that we create our reality 100% and that most likely we are the one who fell short, not the Divine.

The access point for the Pulse is the human heart. The heart is like a tuning fork with the ability to sense the particular spectrum of this energy of existence. The primary emotion of love resides in the heart, along with its yin and yang of joy and sorrow. As we all know, we come from love with its Beauty and Goodness, we are going back to love, we are made of love, and everything is about love. Ultimately, all we need is love, because love is the highest emotional Resonance that links us to the Pulse.

Sadly, many of us don't know how to love or be loved. We need to consciously and continuously learn and practice them both, with awareness that we may well fall short, make mistakes, and get hurt along the way. The more we practice loving and being loved, the more we will need to empty and release sorrow and grief through forgiveness and letting go, because, inevitably, there will be a myriad of things we will feel sorry about. However, as we have said, this is not a fruitless, masochistic process, as the more we empty out our sorrows, the more space we make available for the next level: joy — the ultimate healer.

Love is very hard for most of us to define. It is a skill, an area of expertise, which, as we said, needs to be learned and practiced, always evolving and growing. In our modern-day culture, "love" is often a throwaway, overused and abused term and it can appear to have lost its true meaning. The only truly soul-satisfying definition of love that we have found is from Lazaris, who shares that there are seven actions to take, each of which will produce one of seven feelings or states of being. The seven actions of love are: giving, respecting (honoring the emotions), responding or taking responsibility for, trusting, knowing, being intimate, and caring. These actions need to create one or more of these seven states of being, like security, honesty, pleasure, trust, reduced fear of loss, intimacy, and caring. These seven actions and the seven feelings or states of being then combine to form forty-nine ways of loving and being loved.

In the early days of our relationship, with this formula of love deeply embedded in our hearts and minds, Rowan and I would regularly discuss each of these actions and feelings. In this way, we explored and practiced our love for one another, wanting every aspect of our alliance to grow and evolve.

Love is at the core of any relationship — and all of our relationships are created in order for us to practice the act or art of loving. Firstly, we practice a relationship with our parents, then our siblings and other family members, our friends and our peers at school, and then our first love, our partner, our own children, and so on. And, of course, we continually develop the most essential loving relationship, which is with ourselves. This process of learning and practicing the art of love in different forms of relationships continues throughout our lives, preparing us for the ultimate relationship — with the Pulse, God/Goddess, All That Is.

Every single one of us, whether or not we are aware of it, has a relationship with the Pulse; we are all created from Beauty, Goodness, and Truth. By developing and becoming conscious of this connection, we can move it to the level of Partnership. In this union, the Pulse is our involved and active partner, willing to participate with us 100% in every aspect of our lives.

We know we are working in Partnership with the Pulse when we become aware of changes in our lives that reveal to us — without any shadow of doubt — that we are no longer "flying solo." The Beauty of this union is that the unexpected is a constant companion and we begin to live with the powerful awareness that anything can happen.

Allow your awareness and senses to open, as the signs of your Partnership may be sent to you in any number of different formats. Imagine, for example, that you are pondering a question or wondering about a decision; the answer you're seeking might come via a friend you're talking to about a totally unrelated topic or on the page of a book you open at random or when you find yourself suddenly tuning in to the words of a song or a TV show.

As your Partnership grows, more and more beautiful instances of synchronicity and serendipity will occur in your life, making you smile and sending little shivers down your spine. The more you are aware, the more you will notice your connection and your world will simultaneously feel both magical and miraculous.

As we were given the ultimate gift of free will, no one is allowed or able to interfere in your reality without your asking for help. However, once the covenant of Partnership has been signed, you are working together — and support is always on its way or at hand, without you having to send out any specific request.

The Pulse is a gentle energy, nurturing and nudging you lovingly along your path. Rather than teaching you the hard way "for your own good," via pain and punishment, sadism or suffering, it assists you on your journey with compassionate and loving support. This is how you will be able to recognize its involvement and your connection.

Last year, I was at a conference in Boston. At the end of one particular day, I felt weighed down with pain in my back and had no idea how I would be able to manage the rest of the week. I asked for help to ease my pain. Promptly forgetting this, I continued with my evening. Everything seemed like it was against me; I found myself getting more and more frustrated and angry, as I was repeatedly having to walk an extra few blocks to find each of my destinations, thanks to bad directions and taxi drivers who seemed not to know their own city. It was not until later that night as I was going to bed that I realized I was no longer in pain and that all the extra walking had been the Goddess's way of helping me. Feeling humbled, silly, and laughing out loud, I closed my eyes and silently thanked her.

Imagine for a moment, the enormous benefit of a working partnership with God. You might compare it to suddenly teaming up with a high-level business partner, who immediately and effortlessly affords you access to unforeseen resources and an impressive list of contacts. To enter this realm of miracles, you must align yourself to the Resonance of the transcendent qualities — Beauty, Goodness, and Truth. Then, as miracle after miracle unfolds before your eyes, you feel their divine presence permeating your reality. The presence of the miraculous lifts you to a whole new level of gratitude and appreciation. One of the qualities of appreciation is seeing the wonder in everyone and everything, everywhere.

The task of Emotional Alchemists is to ally themselves with the Pulse, as they work to co-create their reality with this unique support. As a source of energy, insight, and inspiration, the Pulse is second to none. As one forms an inner bond with this power, via reflection, meditation, and visualization, a variety of beneficial qualities naturally arise. To realize this Partnership, the individual must come to co-exist with a level of consciousness higher than the conscious ego. This perspective then becomes the foundation for all external alliances. Only with higher consciousness can our work be in service to something greater than ourselves.

This is what the Merchant Priests in ancient Egypt were trained to do. After completing their training, they went out into the world in service to their communities and humanity at large, maintaining a Partnership with the Pulse. A sense of elegance, ease, and excellence accompanied their movements within society. There was no trace of the attitude of martyrdom that we see in many of the service and helping professions throughout our history and today.

During periods when the Merchant Priests ascended to prominence, they were the most revered class of priests, not unlike our honored PhDs of today. Through participation and their literal partnering with the Pulse, they enjoyed their life's purpose of lifting humanity into Abundance, Peace, and Prosperity. This unique Partnership allowed them to conduct their affairs in the zone of the miraculous. They were awake and full of wonder at the majesty of existence, beyond anything that expectation and imagination might lead one to believe.

Emotional Alchemy alone is a phenomenal resource, but when combined with a direct Partnership with the Pulse, the tectonic plates of your reality will truly begin to shift. If our own experience — as well as that of our close friends, who have also taken up this path — is any indication, you are in for a thrilling ride, whereby *life becomes art*.

GRATITUDE: THE MAGIC OF RECEIVING

NOW THAT WE ARE WORKING IN ALLIANCE WITH OUR ROOT emotions, resonating with the energy and frequency of love and joy, and co-creating in Partnership with the Pulse, everything starts to flow more magically and miraculously in our lives. In this state, we are filled with an overwhelming sense of gratitude and appreciation.

Imagine what it is like to strike an unexpected business deal or come up with an innovation that will benefit hundreds of thousands of people. Or calling a meeting between opposing parties in a hostile take-over situation and finessing a solution, which rallies all involved around an unexpected collaboration and brings out each person's unique strength. When we tap into the Zone and reach a higher order or new synthesis in business, we have the Midas touch that turns dross into pure gold. In these moments, we know that the success is not ours alone. To touch this level is simultaneously humbling and exhilarating. A profound gratitude washes over us and we look skyward with a smile and a wink, knowing we have just had the honor of co-creating with the Pulse. The more this happens, the more we feel a deep appreciation, adding value to everything we create, touch, or do.

Being in the Zone in this way, whatever the context — the athlete moving beyond his former limitations to new heights of performance or musicians playing together, where suddenly everything falls into place and the music seems heaven-sent — in these moments, we are "one with the Pulse" and the resulting feeling state is immense gratitude and appreciation. The crowds shower the athlete or the musicians with their appreciation and the individual feels profoundly grateful.

To feel grateful is to be "full of greatness." In a moment of gratitude, we become greater and more valuable than the individual we are. We become the living, breathing frequency of appreciation. Everything we see or touch increases in value. When, for example, we appreciate, honor, and love our property, blessing it with our gratitude and appreciating it for the security and comfort it offers us, it simultaneously appreciates in value. As the energies lift to gratitude, anything we touch rises in value, anything we do rises in value, and anybody we love, their value similarly expands and grows.

Our dear friend, Dr. Christopher Hills, once carried out a beautiful experiment on the plant kingdom, using the energy of appreciation. On the deck in front of his house, he had a collection of around fifty potted rose bushes, which he adored, arranged on a number of different shelves. Every morning, he would choose the one he felt needed the most appreciation, then move it to the top shelf and spend some time with it, appreciating its Beauty. The rose — in response — would bloom and flourish.

Gratitude is the awareness and acknowledgment that life is far bigger than our individual selves and that we exist in

every moment by virtue of forces far beyond our understanding. Intrinsic to this is our ability to notice the wonder
of life in the small moments, as well as the great ones. The
most seemingly insignificant detail — a chance phone call,
an unexpected opportunity, the door that opened when we
thought it might close — all bring forward deep gratitude.

Everything that enters our life has its own place, even
if we don't know right away what that place is. Gratitude
generates a flow of energy and warmth from each of us
to everyone and everything for which we are thankful and
appreciative, allowing genuine communication and heartfelt
connection. It also keeps us in the benevolent care of humility and is the key to our ability to receive.

Many of us have been taught not to receive, often finding it a difficult or uncomfortable experience. We may feel
guilty or undeserving or fear that we are weak or that we
will owe something in return. However, receiving is the
higher octave of giving.

When you give someone a gift and they genu-
inely receive it, they shower you with appreciation and
gratitude and you, in turn, feel doubly gifted. The gra-
ciousness with which they receive your gift is thrilling and
hugely pleasurable.

To feel true gratitude, we need to know how to gen-
uinely receive and, equally important, we need to *allow*
ourselves to receive. These are vital steps on our Magical
Hero's Journey, which we need to learn and practice. The
more we feel gratitude, the more reasons we have to feel it!

As we join in a more conscious Partnership with the
Pulse, we are able to create things far beyond what we could
create on our own. Once we become adept at consciously

creating magical realities and miracles in our lives (a potential that each and every one of us has within us), we can rest in a state of continual appreciation and wonder. This engages our soul and spirit in a whole new way and stirs up a special kind of allure, activating all our centers, as we become something more than we were before.

Recently, I was driving in my car, contemplating an issue that had been on my mind for many days. I had been looking at it from all perspectives and been unable to come up with an answer to my predicament that was satisfactory to me.

I could feel an anger rising within me. As I drove, I found myself looking heavenward and I shouted: "Come on, WHERE ARE YOU?" To my amazement, almost instantly, an incredible answer came into my mind, an answer that was beyond my view or imagination. I felt an overwhelming sense of gratitude; a mixture of love and joy that literally gave me a warm, fuzzy feeling in my heart, where every cell in my body was enjoying the high from the realization.

Although I had felt thankful and grateful before, I have never consciously felt its movement inside of me. I can only call this feeling sincere gratitude. Its effervescence pulled me into a state of wonder and I said out loud, joyously and sincerely, "WOW! Thank you."

As our throat center or fifth Chakra is activated, the voice gives expression to appreciation and gratitude, further extending the Resonance we feel in our heart.

From this sense of gratitude, we move into a state of wonder, reawakening or unleashing a most beautiful and magical part of ourselves, which has been dormant or denied for so long: the Magical Child.

REAWAKENING THE
MAGICAL CHILD

THE MORE WE CO-CREATE WITH THE PULSE, THE MORE appreciation we feel for the world around us and everyone and everything in it — and the more we enter the "WOW" state of mind, a magical, child-like state of open-eyed wonder.

Do you remember the saying: "Come to God as a child"? Although I understand the meaning of these words now, they used to confuse me when I was younger, as I was not paying attention to the difference between being "childish" and being "child-like."

One of the most important steps on your Hero's Journey is to reawaken your connection with the Magical Child within you, to complete the journey. By connecting with your Magical Child, you open a gateway that invites and allows you to be born again — deleting the past and starting afresh — induced by wonder in major and minor ways, every single day.

Wonder creates a state where all the senses light up; as if "born again," our soul and spirit are called to marvel. Wonder is a form of curiosity, infused with innocence and the sense of mystery we feel after witnessing something magical or miraculous.

Thomas Armstrong, PhD, Executive Director of the American Institute for Learning and Human Development, describes wonder as "the natural astonishment that children and adolescents have about the world around them. Most of us, at one time or another in our youth, have lain on our backs looking up at the sky on a starry night wondering how far the universe went on. This kind of experience reveals the dual meaning of wonder: as a verb ('I wonder how far it goes on') and as an emotional experience ('Wow! It just goes on and on... !')... Wonder doesn't show up as a 'skill' on any competency checklist and thank goodness it doesn't; for by measuring some things we destroy them. But wonder nevertheless is a component of genius."

For the Magical Child, everything is magical. William Blake encapsulated this in the first verse of his poem "Auguries of Innocence": "To see a world in a grain of sand/ And a heaven in a wild flower,/ Hold infinity in the palm of your hand/ And eternity in an hour."

You can explore this for yourself. Hold a piece of wood or a pebble in your hand — or something from the natural world you feel drawn to — and allow yourself to be absorbed in its texture, its density, and the way it fits into your palm. Let the feel, the look, and the smell erase all other thoughts in your mind. Imagine what has gone before and experience the miracle of its creation, knowing you too are a miracle, made of the same energetic material — as is everyone and everything around you.

Now you are living in the field of wonder and awe. You take the time to smell the rain as you step out of the door in the morning and it stops you in your tracks. You see the sunrise and sunset, aware that it is unique every single time.

In winter, in the middle of the city, you stop and breathe in the glorious scent of country air. You begin to really taste the food that you eat, pausing between mouthfuls and suddenly noticing the plethora of flavors that have just hit your palate. You revel in the tingling, the savoring, and the warmth of everything within your world. Wonder is the womb where Beauty is conceived.

The Magical Child is that part of you that was — and still is — "one with all"; one with God/Goddess, one with nature, and one with the universe. Oneness is one of the Magical Child's most beautiful qualities. This is the part of you that existed before it encountered the "Ego I" or "Self I." This is where the separation from God/Goddess originated and where you became disconnected from "All That Is," finding yourself in the wilderness.

Observing and playing with my son Azlan in the first two years of his life, I witnessed how the Magical Child within him was fully flourishing.

As soon as the "terrible twos" began, Azlan's sense of individuality and separation emerged and I noticed him slowly starting to lose his sense of "oneness" and gain his sense of self. He began to call himself "Baby," differentiating himself from "Mummy" and "Daddy" and soon he will know himself to be "Azlan." However, as scientists inform us, there is no time and space — they are merely man-made illusions — and this means his Magical Child is still alive within him — as it is within each of us. Maybe your own Magical Child is reading these words with you right now?

Besides the quality or feeling of wonder and "oneness," another quality of the Magical Child is innocence or, as I like to call it, "beautiful innocence," which sadly most of us lose in the process of growing up. When babies arrive on this planet, they are entirely innocent; they have done nothing "wrong"; their records and their slates are clean, innocent of all charges! Oh, how I would love to have a record like this again.

Whoever we are, whatever life we have led, we all have things that we would like to release and move beyond. Although it is not possible for us to return to our original "clean slate" state, attaining a certain level of childlike innocence is entirely within our reach.

One way to achieve this is through genuine and sincere forgiveness. Many of us feel that forgiveness only involves forgiving others or asking others to forgive us. However, the central key to forgiveness lies in forgiving ourselves. From here, it is possible to also truly forgive others and receive the forgiveness of others.

Although we may never really forget what has happened, we can forgive the past, releasing it and not allowing it to keep haunting, hurting, or damaging us or anyone else in our lives. The more we express the past and let it go, the more we reawaken that beautiful — albeit matured — sense of innocence.

By regularly forgiving ourselves and emptying out our sorrow, guilt, and pain, we reunite with our lost sense of "beautiful innocence," feeling like we are born again and allowing ourselves to begin our lives afresh.

It is much easier to do this process regularly, as we progress through our lives, rather than having to deal with everything that has built up over decades. Once we live in a society where we all learn and practice Emotional Literacy and Emotional Intelligence and therefore deal with our emotions as they arise, we will no longer be weighed down with massive burdens, leaking our precious energy to the past.

At this point, in my view, psychologists and therapists will need to change the focus of their work. As we, as a global race, become more and more emotionally intelligent, regularly emptying out our sorrows and forgiving ourselves, there will be less and less work for psychologists and psychiatrists to do in their current roles. Therefore, their job will evolve: from fixing energy leakage and healing our pasts to helping us have a positive relationship with our future and holding the highest Resonance. They will be more like "Resonance doctors."

Purity is also a quality of our Magical Child, meaning they are clean, non-polluted and non-contaminated, free of the programming, conditioning, and indoctrination of society, parents, school, work, media, advertising, religion, government, etc. They are not yet aware of any boundaries or limitations or any of the different sets of rules they will encounter later in their lives.

As an adult, it entails determination and effort to become pure again. Although we cannot ever regain our original state of immaculate purity, each of us can do what is within our power to purify ourselves. We have the capacity to challenge what we have been taught and told, deleting that which no longer serves us or is irrelevant to our lives. We then automatically create the space to allow us to consciously upload new programs, data, and information — new beliefs, attitudes, learning, understanding, etc. — which we personally have consciously chosen, allowing a new vision of ourselves to emerge.

How do we reprogram ourselves? One way to move beyond these states of mind and to be able to reprogram those parts no longer needed is via self-reflection, meditating on any beliefs that we feel need changing.

There are many great teachers, authors, psychiatrists, and therapists who have found other ways and techniques for us to use to reprogram ourselves. Luckily, we live in an age where there are many alternatives and there is support out there for each one of us.

The next quality of the Magical Child is humility. We are once again willing to explore the known and the unknown with fresh eyes and ears, allowing people and things to be new, to change, and to be different. Just because it has always been this way, it does not mean that it has to be this way again.

For example, several years ago, I began to notice that each time I met my older son in New York, where he lives, both his mother and I would see him as we did when he was as a teenager or young adult. Our judgments would arise, closely followed by arguments with him, which had a detrimental effect on all of us. I began to be aware that we were being quite arrogant and lacking in humility, for surely he had changed considerably in the last ten years, just as we had done. After this, I began to see him with humility, taking notice of how much he had changed and grown, allowing my image of him to also change. Our relationship then matured from a "father and son" relationship to one between two equal adults, developing into a beautiful friendship.

The next quality of the Magical Child is the ability to be in the present moment; totally in the NOW. This is something that, as an adult, we most likely have trouble with, as most of us are constantly distracted by memories of the past, visions of the future, and thoughts about planning, imagining, dreaming, analyzing, and making lists of things to do, etc. The Magical Child quite naturally and happily inhabits the present, with no concept of yesterday or tomorrow.

Sometimes, when we are doing something we feel passionate about and thoroughly enjoy, we are able to live absolutely in the present moment, when all our focus and attention is absorbed in whatever heartfelt activity we are doing. At times of joy, it is impossible to think of either the past or the future. We are 100% present.

There is a saying that sometimes echoes in my mind: "The past is a memory, the future is a mystery, but today is a gift. That is why it is called the present!"

This leads us to the next quality of the Magical Child, which is the ability to have fun and play wholeheartedly. Just like all children, our Magical Child loves to play and enjoy him- or herself, flowing with ease from one activity to another and infusing nearly everything he or she does with a sense of fun.

In this state of fun, our Magical Child is emotionally fluid, where feelings of anger, jealousy, or fear are transient — expressed quickly and then gone. At this stage in our Magical Child's life, he or she has not been programmed to ignore, suppress, or resist his or her emotions. Therefore, our Magical Child flows from one feeling to another, entirely naturally, without any preconceived notions or inhibitions.

Being with my son and learning so much from him has confirmed to me that anyone can be a teacher in our lives — and that everyone and everything that crosses our path may have an important message for us, where we will learn something needed on our journey.

Curiosity is another quality of the Magical Child. I often hear people using the expression "Curiosity killed the cat" — and I respond with my own version: "Curiosity *filled* the cat." Our son is always asking Rowan and me, "Whazzat?," "Whaziss?" and, when we reply, he responds with "Wow!" or a cheeky smile. His inquisitiveness about life is insatiable; he wants to learn and soak up as much information from as many sources as possible.

A sense of innocent curiosity is definitely something we as adults need to rekindle in our lives, reigniting our desire to ask questions and discover more of who we are.

Albert Einstein similarly and elegantly encapsulated the essence of this quality, when he said: "We do not grow old, no matter how long we live. We never cease to stand like curious children before the great mystery into which we were born."

Trust is an important quality of the Magical Child. Our son has 100% trust in Rowan and me. He will throw himself into our arms and know, without any doubt, that we will safely catch him. Sadly, as adults, many of us have been betrayed and severely hurt and have lost our ability to fully trust — in other people, in ourselves, and in the process of life. Fearing that our trust will once again be abused or lacking faith in our own judgment, we can find ourselves leading insular lives, locked away from the full spectrum of what life has to offer. Clearly, we can never be told to trust; it is something that we need to learn how to develop, practice, and sincerely feel.

And finally, the Magical Child embodies the quality of an incredible imagination and the ability to daydream. A connection with our personal internal fantasy world — or "fantasia" — activates an instant gateway to our inspiration, originality, and inventiveness, allowing us to envision, visualize, and create.

As we reawaken our Magical Child, we are able to put the different qualities together within ourselves, reclaiming our magic, our divinity, and our birthright.

Remember: Every single one of us was once a Magical Child and this aspect of ourselves still lives within us. All that has happened is that over the years, we have lost our connection with it or chosen to muzzle, ignore, or suppress it. The Magical Child yearns to be reawakened, unleashed, and set free to live life to the fullest — and to join you on the last leg of your sacred journey: the pursuit of Beauty, Goodness, and Truth.

BEAUTY, GOODNESS, AND TRUTH:
—— THE ETERNAL VERITIES ——

WHEN YOUR LIFE IS FILLED WITH JOY, APPRECIATION, AND wonder, the Beauty of the world falls open before you like a book. The reality of the world — as the manifestation of the Pulse — is Beauty, Goodness, and Truth, known throughout history as the "Eternal Verities." This is who we are. This is what everything is. There is only this. It is the ultimate realization of humanity and the path of the Merchant Priesthood, past and present.

A deep understanding of this concept first burst into my own awareness in 1998, when I was meditating at an event along with three hundred other people at the Holiday Inn at Los Angeles International Airport. The point of the meditation was to experience the birth of the universe firsthand. Science hypothesizes that with the "Big Bang," the universe was born. Subatomic particles emanating from this cosmic explosion filled the vast reaches of space, becoming neutrons, protons, and photons, then atoms and molecules, until these formations of early matter evolved into rocks, vegetables, animals and, eventually, humans.

In my vision that day, which has never left me, I experienced a romantic version of the Big Bang. Although I strongly believe that the Divine or Eternal is indivisible and is "One" with no gender, I saw the Goddess in all her glory seduce God; the two made love — and "Bang!" The ecstasy generated by this glorious union seeded the universe with infinite units of consciousness of which I was — and am — one. As the universe was born, every molecule and atom carried the masculine fire or vital energy that we know as light and also the glorious essence of the Goddess. While I was deep in meditation, the Goddess revealed herself to me, as the quintessential expression of Beauty, Goodness, and Truth. This "original essence" registered in my awareness as the most exquisite and gentle vibration imaginable, pulsing in the core of my being and throbbing throughout my entire body. Recognizing that this is what gave birth to all function and form, I fully accepted the invisible trinity of Beauty, Goodness, and Truth as our essence. Everybody and everything is Beautiful, Good, and True. This is what scripture points to with expressions such as: "You are made in the image and likeness of God."

I was left with the exquisite Resonance of "knowingness without certainty," often referred to as faith. I realized that our spiritual journey is to remember the Truth of who we are, experience our own Goodness, and become Beautiful. Our purpose can then be seen as a "holy opportunity" to realize and express this trinity, which is both our heritage and our birthright. Although the setting of a busy airport hotel in Los Angeles was a far cry from the "mountaintop," I had the sense that I had glimpsed the eternal. From then on, this divine triad became the driving force guiding me in my life.

Philosophers and sages the world over have been aware of this knowledge for thousands of years. Socrates was the first person in the West to name these eternal verities, but they are to be found at the heart of every great religious tradition and even the most hardcore atheist would agree with them. In Islam, Truth (Haqq), Beauty (Jamat), and the Good (Birr) are divine names and attributes of God. In his blog, Canadian bishop Thomas Dowd eloquently relates how they harmonize and resonate with the three great Christian virtues: faith, hope, and love.

Faith is the virtue connected to Truth — and its human receptor is the mind or reason. Faith is not merely blind belief, but rather a choice to trust. We look for Truth, often testing it first and the more we see it manifesting in our lives, the more we trust it, until the choice to trust becomes almost automatic. Faith in the Divine works similarly: it is the "knowingness without certainty" that God exists. Our approach to God involves a genuine seeking for *truth about God*. Faith grows as our quest for the ultimate truth continues, developing into a spontaneous habit of trust in God — the basis of any true relationship and partnership.

Hope is the virtue connected to Beauty and for this, the human receptor is the imagination. Hope rides on the wings of Beauty, because Beauty has the capacity to lift us out of whatever situation we are in with an experience of ecstasy, or *ek-stasis*, (the original Greek term), which literally means "to be beside yourself." Hope is vibrant with positive expectation and anticipation — and is the echo that remains, when the experience of ecstasy has passed.

In the presence of something truly beautiful, we might gasp, whistle, clap, or simply silently admire. As we are drawn into a state of contemplation, time itself can appear to stop. Ordinary life is all too often filled with useless distractions and sufferings, but it all evaporates like mist when Beauty appears, guiding us to reconnect with the true meaning of our humanity.

This brings us to the greatest virtue of all: Love. Love is connected to Goodness and conscience is the receptor allowing us to experience it. The philosophical category of the good is broad indeed, but for our purposes, it is easiest to focus on one small aspect, namely "moral Goodness." Simply put, there is a general human preference to be associated with good people rather than evil ones. However, even when we do freely associate with evil people, it is because we see some good in them, which we want to be a part of or possibly encourage.

Being around evil people raises tension — and being subject to evil acts and choices breeds hatred. On the other hand, being in the presence of moral Goodness is profoundly satisfying and, when we choose to become agents of Goodness, it is heartwarmingly rewarding. In this context, Love means a desire to work for the good of others, which leads to the discovery that we are also achieving something good for ourselves. Love — or virtue — becomes its own reward.

Each of the three eternal verities is a Resonance. Beauty, for example, is a transcending energy that can instantly lift us out of the ordinary world. In the presence of Beauty, we don't need to go through the steps of transmuting anger to courage and then to passion. Our anger simply vanishes, as if it were never there in the first place.

Let's say you get into a disagreement with someone you're close to, for example, your partner or your best friend. You walk out of the house angry as heck, slamming the door. Driving away, you see that the sun is beginning to set and you stop to watch the gorgeous pink, crimson, and flaming orange colors splashed across the sky. In an instant, you transcend your feelings of anger and rage and get a glimpse of the other person's point of view. As you stand in awe of life's Beauty, passion fills your heart and your anger disappears. You didn't need to process it, you didn't need to figure it out, you didn't need to talk to anyone, the feeling simply vanished.

Lazaris defines Beauty as a Resonance comprising four pairs of feelings or frequencies. The first two frequencies are joy and peace. Usually, these feelings are not felt at the same time. Joy is masculine and very active, peace is feminine and passive and it would seem they cancel each other out. However, when we are in the presence of Beauty, looking at the sunset, for example, we can experience joy and peace simultaneously. The same is equally true for the other pairs — serenity and exhilaration, majesty and wonder, enchantment and inspiration — each being a harmonious partnership of the masculine and the feminine. When all four pairs or eight frequencies combine, they come together to create a Resonance that is far more powerful than the sum of its components: Beauty.

The more we allow our own Beauty to shine through, the more we choose to create Beauty. And the more we see the Beauty in everything, the closer we resonate with — and are in alignment with — the Pulse.

In the realm of Beauty, everything is transcended. The portal to the miraculous opens. We move with excellence and elegance. With the least amount of energy spent, we achieve the maximum results. Using intentional focus, we can learn to harness ecstasy and Beauty, as a way to transcend the past.

Many years ago, I used to feel angry at friends of mine who would go to India, find a guru or a teacher, and would then call me to say, "Oh, I had the most incredible experience. I sat down with my guru and my problems disappeared." "What?" I would reply. "Your problems suddenly, instantly disappeared? You must be kidding me. Do you really believe your problems just melted away, because you sat down with a guru?" My logic and reason couldn't handle the idea of this at all. However, now I'm able to understand what happened to my friends; they sat down with the sage or teacher of their choosing and, in their presence, they attuned to the Resonance of Beauty. They simultaneously felt joy and peace, stillness and excitement, the wonder and the majesty — and this lifted them to a place where all their problems disappeared.

Our highest aspiration on the path of Sacred Commerce —.just as it was for the Merchant Priests — is to see the beautiful in everything and everyone, to always create the beautiful, and to become more and more beautiful every day.

As Rowan would tell you, she sees me as "75% beautiful," embodying six of the eight frequencies that make up Beauty. She doesn't mean that I have a perfect "ten out of ten" rating on each of those six frequencies; I simply have enough for them to be recognized. When she is in my presence, Rowan feels joy and exhilaration, enchantment and inspiration, majesty and wonder, but not necessarily a feeling of peace and serenity. This shows me exactly what I need to work with on my path to becoming a more beautiful person, resonating more strongly with the Divine.

How beautiful are you?

Rowan possesses the amazingly heartwarming quality of being able to see the Beauty in everyone. We'll be walking together somewhere and suddenly she'll say, "Wow! Look how beautiful that person is." She sees the person's inner Beauty, regardless of his or her appearance or status: the Beauty in an old man's eyes, the smile of a shy young girl, the warmth of a mother's embrace. Although I have more of a tendency to look at appearances, to judge and analyze people, trying to figure them out and put them in a box, I am learning from Rowan's example to search for people's intrinsic Beauty.

The Merchant Priests' embodiment of the Resonance of Beauty enabled them to help humanity to magically transcend their problems or issues. Similarly, the Knights Templar traveled across Europe, building some of the most stunningly beautiful churches in the world, with the intention of uplifting people's Resonance, so they might transcend their troubles.

Some of the most well-known facts about the Knights Templar are that they protected pilgrims as they journeyed to the Holy Land, performed secret rituals, built beautiful churches, and answered only to the pope. However, although the Knights appeared on the surface to be in service to the church, they were actually much more in tune with the Divine feminine. Their underlying objective was to assist the worshippers in transcending their suffering and pain, via exposure to incredible Beauty.

When in church, the worshippers believed that the sense of peace they experienced was as a direct result of the prayers they had chanted, the sermon they had listened to, or the sins they had confessed. However, the shift in their Resonance was often due to their exposure to the sacred and beautiful Resonance of the church building itself. The high-ranking Knights Templar, the designers of the churches, had access to the rarified knowledge of sacred geometry and architecture and acute awareness of the transcendent quality of Beauty. It was as if they literally created "*transcending machines.*"

The path of Beauty heralds the embrace of both the sacred and the feminine side of human nature. At this point in our collective and cultural evolution, the "return of the feminine" is widely regarded as quintessential to our next evolutionary step. The feminine is present in all people, regardless of gender.

The patriarchal system of the last few thousand years has served its purpose in bringing forth many important advances, which may not have otherwise occurred, enabling the development of agriculture, the founding of cities, the development of institutions, and the rule of law. However, we are now entering a new dawn of the human race, where new qualities and organizing/disorganizing principles are required.

Like Beauty, Goodness is another transcending energy. Many people have defined the qualities or virtues of Goodness, but my preference is to equate it with the qualities of chivalry, as delineated in the map of Merlin and King Arthur, where each knight of the Round Table embodied a specific chivalrous quality.

When we meet somebody and think, "Wow, what a *good* person," what we are sensing is that he or she is encapsulating many of the qualities of chivalry: honor, loyalty, nobility, virtue, grace, trust, courage, courtesy, gallantry, authority, ser-vice, and humility. The resonance of these twelve qualities is vastly greater than the sum of the parts; the frequencies automatically lift us to a higher octave of being.

In meditation, you can practice imagining each of the qualities of Goodness and what they feel like for you — and simultaneously, your brain will secrete chemical after chemical into your physiological system, eliciting an alchemical reaction.

As there are twelve qualities, you could choose to explore one a month for a year. Observe the quality — in yourself and in others; be aware of it; research it; practice it; change some habits; do some exercises; ask your friends and family how you're doing, etc. By exploring and prac-ticing each one of the twelve qualities and bringing them into your consciousness and awareness, you are drawing the qualities of Goodness to you. Your goal is to massage and refine each quality, allowing the alchemical response to flow, creating a Resonance of Goodness.

Always begin your creative programming process by putting yourself in a bubble of Beauty, Goodness, and Truth. It's great to have a high Resonance and sharpened hooks, but it is also essential to have the right energy to get them moving. For this you need your highest Resonance — and there is nothing higher than Beauty, Goodness, and Truth.

As with Beauty, the Merchant Priests always saw the Goodness in everyone and everything, their actions were sourced in Goodness, and they always felt their innate Goodness. This is something we should endeavor to emu-late. Even the worst criminal in jail — or the most evil person — has Goodness inside of them. Remember, we are all made out of Beauty, Goodness, and Truth.

Researching the meaning of Truth, it is possible to find so many different definitions, postulated by both modern and ancient philosophers, we can be left feeling confused and overwhelmed. For thousands of years, the debate, disagreement, and discussion surrounding the question "What is Truth?" have continued unabated. Is it subjective or objective? Relative or absolute? Minimalist or pluralist? Etc.

In the context of the Hero's Journey, we want to keep things simple, practical, and useful, so we define Truth as "knowledge"; specifically, the knowledge about how nature and the universe functions: the universal laws of the universe.

One of the highest truths is that we create our own reality, 100% — either by causing it or attracting it. If, for example, we walk under a bridge and a stone falls on our head, we might say, "I didn't cause this to happen. How could I create this?" However, we must ask ourselves why we happened to pass under the bridge at that exact moment when the stone fell? We *chose* to walk under that particular bridge at that particular time when that particular stone was falling. We might not have caused this event, but when we explore this situation in more depth, we will find, on a certain level, a certain element of our Resonance attracted this event into our lives.

Another truth is that "we are all one." To imagine ourselves to be separate is a delusion — albeit one that still perpetuates within some people's belief systems.

Sometimes, I walk down the street and I practice the following exercise: I look at each person I meet, whether they are a man, a woman, or a child, and I say to myself, "Wow! This is me." I sit on the train and I look at my fellow travelers and I say to myself, "Wow! That's me, just in another body. When I look at them, I am also looking at me" — and I start imagining what it might feel like if I was them.

In meditation, I also imagine myself as the leaves on the tree or as the tree itself or as a bird or an animal or water. By allowing my feelings and imaginings to incubate, I am aware that I am, quite literally, connected to everything. This is the ultimate realization and experience: feeling oneness with everyone and everything.

As we said, we see Truth as knowledge. However, knowledge *without* the benefit of emotions is simply "science." Scientific knowledge can be used to create something beautiful or something destructive. Knowledge *with* emotions is "wisdom."

The direct application of Beauty, Goodness, and Truth in action in the world leads to something even greater — and that "something" is actually a "someone." Even as our deepest spiritual aspirations draw us into Beauty, Goodness, and Truth, we cannot stop there, because even these virtues will just become another religious system — and we simply become an insignificant part of that larger system. No, the ultimate way to live the qualities of Beauty, Goodness, and Truth is in a relationship with another person, not necessarily in a marriage or sexual union, but someone in our life, who is as interested in developing the qualities as we are ourselves.

The eternal verities are not ultimate realities; they point to that which is beyond them: the Divine. God is not a symbol of Goodness. Goodness is a symbol of God. Each member of this trinity — Beauty, Goodness, and Truth — is a symbol, a signifier, which tells us something about the Divine. This is the real reason we should pursue them and draw them into our lives. The Divine is not beautiful — the Divine *is* Beauty. All that is beautiful somehow reflects the Divine, as an icon, a doorway for us to walk through to the wordless, formless Beauty, which is beyond all earthly forms and yet, paradoxically, is within them.

Take some time to think about the public figures considered to be both respected and highly evolved human beings. Consider Nelson Mandela (who passed away during the writing of this edition), Desmond Tutu, and His Holiness, the Dalai Lama. Each of them epitomizes the qualities of Beauty, Goodness, and Truth.

Today's Knights of Commerce know that Heaven and Earth are one and the same, just as they know that form and the formless interpenetrate each other and are also one and the same. The Merchant Priests, both the ancient and the modern, served and serve something infinitely greater than themselves: greater than anything that can be given a name. Yet at the same time, they are completely at home in the everyday affairs of human exchange and interaction. They know we are all in this together, that nothing is separate from anything else and, therefore, everything — every single word, gesture, transaction, thought, and feeling — matters.

Today's Global Citizens recognize this time as the age of *party-cipation*, in which we all play a part and we are all invited to the party — to learn and to grow into the Divine together. Like the man or woman who has been "born again," the new Global Citizens shed their old skin — the "I" and the "me," the first primitive individualism that was useful for a time — and are reborn as new people, who recognize their intrinsic unity with everyone and everything that lives and breathes.

In this new *Age of Party-cipation*, we come to the Divine with eyes and arms open, ready to dive in up to our elbows, if that is what is needed. We don't have to sit in a cave for thirty years to become enlightened, we can do it right here in the modern marketplace, learning to activate our true Partnership with the Pulse. Our calling now is to be co-creators: co-creators with each other, but above all, co-creators with the Divine.

Beauty, Goodness, and Truth are Resonances, which, when combined, create something far greater than the sum of their constituents: ecstasy, a state of being that accompanies enlightenment — the pinnacle of the Sacred Hero's Journey.

As we develop our Resonance, we will begin to feel the five qualities of ecstasy emerge into our lives: we are filled with joy, feeling fully at peace; we feel a sense of happiness and expectation and are fully accepting of ourselves; we are filled with awe and majesty, fully able to soar and be carefree; we are filled with love and feel fully loved; we live in a state of euphoria, where everything has a glow, a radiance, and God/Goddess/All That Is dwells everywhere, even in the space between spaces.

As we pursue Beauty, Goodness, and Truth, we begin to feel and experience instances — explosions — of ecstasy, which, as we progress along our journey, become more and more frequent. The steps of getting there are the qualities of being there.

EPILOGUE:
HERALDING THE AGE OF
CONSCIOUSNESS

"But Sir Launcelot rode overthwart and endlong in a wild
forest and held no path, but as wild adventure led him."
— "THE QUEST OF THE SANGREAL"
FROM *Age of Chivalry*, BY THOMAS BULFINCH

HUMANITY HAS JOURNEYED FROM THE STONE AGE, TO THE
Bronze Age, all the way to the Age of Agriculture, the
Industrial Revolution, and more recently the Information Age.

We are now at the beginning of the next big era of
human evolution, the *Age of Consciousness*. We are referring
to the deepening sense of being present to the mystery and
wonder of being alive — knowing that a much greater force
of creative intelligence is working with and through us. It is
about being aware of the bigger picture and the connection
between all things. Where in times past the pursuit of higher
consciousness was restricted to the very few, in the Age of
Consciousness it is available to everyone — just as in the
Age of Information everything you wanted to know was at
your fingertips.

In each of the ages, Commerce has been a prevalent
force. During the Age of Agriculture, those who owned the

land and the agricultural tools and machinery prospered. The same is true for the Information Age. Individuals and businesses who helped you search, store, and disseminate information became the largest and most influential companies — i.e. IBM, Cisco, Apple, Google, Facebook, etc.

In this new Age of Consciousness, individuals and businesses who are creating products, content, and services that raise consciousness will be the ones who will lead and evolve our culture, economy, ecology, spirituality, and government. This is what Sacred Commerce is all about.

Many of you have been the heralds of this emerging Age of Consciousness. For years and decades you have invested in yourselves, your skills, and your businesses. Your time has come! What a joy and a privilege it is to witness and party-cipate in the birth of a new humanity.

ABOUT THE AUTHORS

AYMAN SAWAF is an international visionary entrepreneur, published musician, and best-selling author. He is one of the original creators of the discipline now known as Emotional Literacy (EL). He is also an early pioneer in Emotional Intelligence (EI or "EQ") as co-creator of the Four Cornerstone Model and its application in business — as illustrated in *Executive EQ: Emotional Intelligence in Leadership and Organizations*, which Ayman co-authored with Dr. Robert Cooper. He has spent the last twenty years building the evolutionary foundation for entirely new systems and industries that will monetize the ability of these perspectives to optimize human capital; by providing new maps to evolve our relationships with ourselves, our family, and the workplace.

AymanSawaf.com and AymanMusic.com

ROWAN GABRIELLE is a visionary artist, entrepreneur, and philanthropist with 20+ years experience in the conscious marketplace. She is the founder of OrganicLeather.com, a company focused on Eco-Fashion and revolutionizing our relationship to animals and the clothes we wear. She is deeply passionate about spirituality and inter-species communication, a connector with deep relationships across many subject areas. She is also a special event producer and a photographer.

RowanGabrielle.com